TIER 1

Christianity

THE STORIES, LESSONS, AND HEROES OF THE
SPECIAL OPERATIONS COMMUNITY.

THE GOSPEL OF JESUS, AND THE JOURNEY OF
DISCIPLESHIP

by

DREW ALAN HALL

ISBN 979-8-88616-622-4 (paperback)
ISBN 979-8-88751-819-0 (hardcover)
ISBN 979-8-88616-623-1 (digital)

Christian Faith Publishing
832 Park Avenue
Meadville, PA 16335
www.christianfaithpublishing.com

Printed in the United States of America

Contents

Mission Briefing

When you hear the term *special operations*, what comes to your mind? In the military, it means the best of the best—a group of elite soldiers who are the most dangerous fighting force on planet Earth. Maybe you think of that awesome movie you watched where guys jump out of planes, repel off the side of buildings, or sneak in to take out the bad guy in the middle of the night. Whatever it is, I am sure you have a mental picture right now. The truth is, these are soldiers who go above the call of being a soldier. I believe that any man or woman who wears the uniform is far from ordinary. Anyone willing to leave their family and friends to go serve the greater good of the country is anything but average. Inside that group is another tier of greatness. Where men go through more training and more demands to separate themselves from the rest. All the pain and punishment for the chance to be a part of the military's elite force carrying out the most dangerous missions of protecting our freedom. When our country needs the best, their phone rings first. The process of becoming one of these elite soldiers has always captivated me. Not only the physical side of training, but what really interests me is the mental side. I have also been inspired by their never-ending commitment to growth. Always striving to be better. From the stories about the action and valor of real American heroes, to the leadership lessons learned from a career in the field of special operations, about half of my personal library is made up of books about special operations.

Ever since I was little, history has always been a passion of mine. One of my favorite childhood memories is talking with my grandfather about World War II. I can remember listening to him tell me all his stories from the war. Every time, every word he spoke captivated my heart and mind. As I got older, that love for history grew. As a history teacher, now in my thirties, I understand the importance of passing on the lessons of history to the next generation. God shows us the importance of understanding history in his word. Romans 15:4 says, "For everything that was written in the past was written to teach us, so that through the endurance taught in the Scriptures and the encouragement they provide we might have hope" (NIV).

I myself have never served in any of the branches of the military. That is an honor that both my grandfathers proudly held, as well as many friends who volunteered to protect our freedom. Everyone who has or will wear that uniform is a hero! I would be lying if I said it was not something that a part of me wanted. I actually tried to enlist at one point in my life. I married the love of my life, and God blessed us with two amazing little girls. I had a good job as a teacher and coach at my alma mater. I was serving as the youth pastor at the church I grew up in. Through different events and circumstances, I began to think maybe God wants me to do something else. I had it in my mind that the National Guard chaplain was my path. Let's call it a midlife identity crisis. I did an internet search and contacted a recruiter, prayed about it for a year, filled out the paperwork, and went to MEPS (Military Entrance Processing Station). MEPS is where they process anyone wanting to join the military. Basically, they see if you qualify physically for the military. When you get done with all the screening, they give you your paperwork to see if you qualify. Everything that is a red flag has a code. My paper looked like I was creating a computer program. Okay, it was not that bad, but I did have some things that disqualified me. So I realized God had a different plan for my life. So this made me really do some soul searching. I had to spend some time with God and ask him what he wanted me to do.

Above anything else, I believe I was created to preach the gospel, teach God's holy, perfect word, and encourage people. My prayer is that I can accomplish all three in this book. It is important to understand God has a specific plan for your life and mine. I just want to step into what God has for me and try to do that at a high level. One of the worship songs that I love is "Shine Like Stars" by Passion music. One of the lyrics is simply this: "I'm gonna burn bright, I got just one life, to shine like stars in the heavens." I hope I can do that in this book. That I can use my one life to shine bright for God and point and encourage people to Jesus. I know that if people open their eyes and hearts to see the King of glory, their lives will never ever be the same!

Through my role in each area of my life, I have seen a problem coming down the line like a locomotive barreling toward a car stuck on the track. Our society is gradually accepting and, in some cases, celebrating mediocrity. If you just show up when you are asked and halfway do your job, you are a great employee. People want more money, more recognition, but less work. The idea of entitlement seems to be woven into more and more people's DNA than ever before. This is reflected in our work ethic as well as our morality and our relationships with others. We are also more disengaged, self-centered, and easily polarized by specific topics.

What is even scarier is that these same issues have infiltrated Christianity. If you attend church two out of four weeks, you are a great church member. We count reading a push notification from the Bible app on our phone as time with God. The job of sharing the gospel is the sole responsibility of ministers and missionaries. The work of the church is placed mostly on the 10 percent of the faithful members. Not only are we average at best in our church attendance, but we are not even close to that at the giving of our time, money, and talent for the glory of God. Think about this for a second. When was the last time someone tried to share the good news of Jesus with you? When was the last time you shared the gospel with someone? Is Hell not real anymore? Did everyone on the planet declare Jesus king and Lord? No, the problem is that the answer to those questions is found in our disengagement or disinterest in the gospel. We love the story of the gospel of Jesus, but do we care about the mission of that same gospel?

That is why I am writing this book. I want to take the passion and interest God has given me and use them to encourage you and to show you God has called you to a life of greatness that can only be found in Jesus. God did not call us too easy or average. He called us to be something special…to a level above what a world bound for hell accepts. I believe that God does not make mistakes and that he has a plan for your life and mine. He wants us to be great in the role he designed us for and deserves at the very least our best! Being a great employee, parent, spouse, friend is one way we glorify God. First Corinthians 10:31 says, "So whether you eat or drink or whatever you do, do it all for the glory of God" (NIV). We don't have to be a part of the story of God… WE ARE ALLOWED TO BE! This is a mindset that we could all benefit from. Just like the old army recruiting phrase, "Be all that you can be in the army," we need to have that same mindset in our Christian life—to be all that we can be for the glory of God.

God wants you to be an asset for him. If you need to hear it in church terms, God wants you to be the best disciple for him that you can be, in the church, in your family, in your job, and in all areas where God has called you to his purpose. An asset is someone who can be counted on. That should be the desire of our heart. I want to strive to be someone God can rely on. I also want my family, friends, and coworkers to be able to depend on me too. The worst thing we can do is be a liability in any or all of those areas in our life. That is not what you are made for!

Remember every member of the special operations community is a volunteer. Each decided to do this out of his or her own free will. No one was forced to take this journey. The same is true of us. No one is forcing you into a relationship with Jesus. It is an open invitation from a God who is in love with you. Who wants to spend time with you and wants to help you grow into the person he designed you to be. We just have to be willing to accept the call. From ordinary sinful people, to the saved and redeemed children of God. We are changed! If you ask me that, transformation is far more extraordinary than anything this world can offer you.

So my hope and prayer is that in this book, I can draw connections between the lessons, heroes, and stories of special operations and the call of being Jesus's disciple. I pray these connections stir your heart to want to grow deeper in your relationship with God. I pray this will speak boldness and courage into your life and propel you to become an asset of Jesus in your job, relationships, passions, and interests. I pray you will have a desire to want to be a part of the hard work of reaching a lost world with the saving grace only found in Jesus. Above anything else, I pray that if you don't know Jesus as your personal savior that through the pages of this book, God will speak to your heart about his love and mercy and grace. Jesus is our way to God, the truth we need in this world, and the life we were created for.

"The thief comes only to steal and kill and destroy. I came' that they may have life and have it abundantly" (John 10:10).

1

Basic Training

Therefore, if anyone is in Christ, he is a new creation. The old has passed away; and behold the new has come.

—2 Corinthians 5:17 (ESV)

Tier 1 assets are at the top of the military's direct action ladder. When the mission is hard, or the situation is tough, they are the military's plan A. No matter what group of tier 1 operators you are talking about (Green Berets, SEALS, PJs, SAS, etc.), they all had to start at the same point, basic training. No matter how great of an athlete or marksman he or she is in the civilian world, every man and woman who joins the military has to start at the bottom.

This is a theme you can see throughout the entirety of the tier 1 pipeline. Everyone starts at the bottom with basic training. Then upon graduation, each man goes right back to the bottom. Most special warfare tracks have a selection process. After selection, however, it is right back to the bottom in the training schools. These processes can take years before they ever reach the status of tier 1 operator. Then once assigned to a team, it is right back to the bottom as "the new guy." Every new stage takes the soldier back to square one. It is safe to say in this line of work, learning never stops.

The ultimate square one of the journey is basic training. The US Army describes basic training as your introduction into army service. No matter what branch of the military you look at, the goal of basic training is to teach recruits the traditions, tactics, and methods of becoming a soldier. It also covers how to live the military life. Basic training shows you how to dress and live out the values of each branch. It also shows you how to perform in the military. Basic covers everything from how to stand, how to march, how to fall in formation, how to shoot, and even how to make your bed. It is the transition from civilian life to military life. Before anyone can become tier 1, they must take step one.

You can Google the different basic training for each individual branch and find all the videos and information you want. Let's take a quick look at the United States Army's basic training. The first phase is for lack of a better word is indoctrination—to take a man or woman from civilian to soldier. They learn core values, how to assemble and disassemble a weapon (if you're like me, you have that scene from the movie *Jarhead* playing in your mind right now: "This is my rifle"), and other basics of army life. The goal is to tear the new soldier down and build each one back up with the framework of discipline and teamwork; the things they will need to be a successful part of any branch of the military that he joins. The second phase covered everything from marksmanship to map and compass reading. Phase 3 looks a lot like phase 2 with different challenges and tests that soldiers must pass. After the completion of all three phases, the only thing left is graduation.

Once each man and woman has completed their basic training, they are different. You could say they are a new creation. No longer the same man or woman, but built up with new values. And walking in new paths from their former life. This is something that must happen. It is not optional for anyone wanting to become a tier 1 asset. They must start at square one. Now square one is in no way intended to be fun. Waking up early every day, running everywhere you go, and getting yelled at for everything are not my ideas of a great ten-week vacation. It is a process, though. There are no Captain America chambers where you insert a soldier, set the timer, and when it goes off, you have a super soldier. Nobody gets to skip to the front of the line. Even the cadets and midshipmen of the service academies go through basic training.

As Christians, Jesus tells us that we all must start at square one. In John's gospel, we see this in chapter 3 where Nicodemus goes to Jesus in John 3:1–21:

> Now there was a Pharisee, a man named Nicodemus who was a member of the Jewish ruling council. He came to Jesus at night and said, "Rabbi, we know that you are a teacher who has come from God. For no one could perform the signs you are doing if God were not with him." Jesus replied, "Very truly I tell you, no one can see the kingdom of God unless they are born again." "How can someone be born when they are old?" Nicodemus asked. "Surely they cannot enter a second time into their mother's womb to be born!" Jesus answered, "Very truly I tell you, no one can enter the kingdom of God unless they are born of water and the Spirit. Flesh gives birth to flesh, but the Spirit gives birth to spirit. You should not be surprised at my saying,

'You must be born again.' The wind blows wherever it pleases. You hear its sound, but you cannot tell where it comes from or where it is going. So it is with everyone born of the Spirit." "How can this be?" Nicodemus asked. "You are Israel's teacher," said Jesus, "and do you not understand these things? Very truly I tell you, we speak of what we know, and we testify to what we have seen, but still you people do not accept our testimony. I have spoken to you of earthly things and you do not believe; how then will you believe if I speak of heavenly things? No one has ever gone into heaven except the one who came from heaven—the Son of Man. Just as Moses lifted up the snake in the wilderness, so the Son of Man must be lifted up, that everyone who believes may have eternal life in him." For God so loved the world that he gave his one and only Son, that whoever believes in him shall not perish but have eternal life. For God did not send his Son into the world to condemn the world, but to save the world through him. Whoever believes in him is not condemned, but whoever does not believe stands condemned already because they have not believed in the name of God's one and only Son. This is the verdict: Light has come into the world, but people loved darkness instead of light because their deeds were evil. Everyone who does evil hates the light, and will not come into the light for fear that their deeds will be exposed. But whoever lives by

the truth comes into the light, so that it may
be seen plainly that what they have done has
been done in the sight of God.

Now you have to understand how radical Jesus's words are to Nicodemus. Nicodemus was part of the Jewish ruling council. He would have known the scriptures and what they said about the coming messiah. He would have known all the laws of Moses and how to live a life pleasing to God. He thought the messiah was coming to deliver them from their oppressors (Rome). Jesus did not come with a military plan to conquer the world for the Jewish people. He came to conquer a bigger enemy—death! Jesus had a reputation already as a teacher or prophet. You see this in the way Nicodemus addresses him at the beginning of chapter 3. Jesus then tells him that if one wants to see the kingdom of God he must be born again, not follow certain laws and traditions, but become something new. Now Nicodemus was an educated man. He knows a person cannot be born again. You see this in his response about crawling back up inside one's mom. So Jesus's response blows his mind. However, Jesus begins to explain to him that you must be born of flesh and spirit. This is something that you cannot do yourself. Just as in our physical birth, our moms did all the work. The same is true with our spiritual birth. God does the work. Nicodemus's life had been spent trying to do everything right. So when Jesus tells him that the way to heaven is completely opposite of everything he built his life on, well, you can understand why he had a problem accepting Jesus's words. God does not leave us wondering, though. Jesus tells him in John 3:16 that God's son does the work of salvation.

Every person is born into sin. You, me, your parents, your neighbor, the waitress at your favorite restaurant, your favorite athlete or artist, all are born into the same problem. This is why

John 3:16 is so beautiful. God loves us so much that he died for us. Not only to forgive us, but most importantly, also to restore our relationship with him. Everyone has the same problem, and God gave everyone the same answer to that problem: Jesus! Think about how awesome that is for a second. The God of the universe who needs and wants for nothing, wants a relationship with you. It means so much to him that he came and took our sin and shame and placed it on his son. Jesus tells us the only step we have to take in the path back to God is to be born again. Now once you are born again, you are adopted into the family of God. John 1:12–13 tells us, "Yet to all who did receive him, to those who believed in his name, he gave the right to become children of God—children born not of natural descent, nor of human decision or a husband's will, but born of God" (NIV). It's like going from civilian life to military life, you are different.

All of this begins with a simple request from Jesus, "Follow me." Now the words are simple, but the weight of them is heavy. So much emotion rushes your heart when you think of it. The son of God, the Messiah, the King of kings, the Lamb who takes away the sin of the world, wants you to follow him. Now if you're like me you probably think all your past mistakes should hold you back. Like Jesus could never use anyone as broken and damaged as me. This is the beauty of it! He asks you right where you are to follow him. He will tear down the things in your life that need to be torn down and build up the things that are of him (Gal. 5:22–26). We only need to accept his invitation. We accept it by believing in him. Believing that he is the Son of God. He is the one who takes away the sin of the world. He did die on a cross and after three days rose from the grave.

Now we have to ask ourselves this question: If we don't believe those things, why would we follow Jesus? A call to take care of the widows, children, and sick people sounds like a noble cause. Something that a good person would do. However, there are a lot of good people who help the needy that don't know Jesus. The sad thing is no matter how much good they do, no matter how many people they help, their sin still separates them from God. Living your life in order to bring glory to a good teacher is noble, but crazy, because that good teacher can't get you to heaven. Since we do believe those things about him, we live to honor Jesus because of who he is and what he did. So as a Jesus's follower, we don't follow Jesus so he will love us. We follow Jesus because he loves us! Remember, our love and good works did not put Jesus on the cross; it was our sin that did that.

Just like in phase 1 of basic training where new soldiers are stripped of the things from their old life and built back up with the core values of the military, Christians need that as well. The Bible calls us a new creation. We need to strip away the things of our old life that are holding us back from our new life with Christ. Take a second before we go any further and think and pray. Ask God what you need to get rid of to make room for what he wants to give you. Maybe it is hate for someone who has done you wrong. Maybe it is jealousy over something or someone. Maybe it's the struggle with lust or maybe you committed adultery. I am not trying to shame you or make you feel bad. I just want you to see that, though, that may have been the old you, it does not need to be a part of the new you. You don't have to or need to bring those things into your new life. Look at them like contraband. That is the term the army uses for anything that a new soldier brings with them to basic training that is not allowed. Once it is found, it is thrown away. So before we go on this journey of following Jesus, we must get rid of the contraband.

Also, just as basic training advances the new soldiers from phase to phase, Christians were meant to advance and grow. It is important to understand Christianity is a way of life, not an event. Have you grown any since surrendering your heart to

God, and making him king of your life or is your walk with Jesus one day where you realized your sin and asked God to save you, but then left it right there? Was your salvation simply an event or a lifestyle? These are tough questions, but important questions that we have to ask ourselves. A relationship with God is not an event, but a lifestyle.

If you look in my closet, you will see a lot of army and navy football shirts and hoodies. My favorite football game of the year is the Army-Navy game. The pageantry of it is second to none. I have always had the utmost respect for the students of the service academies. Where most eighteen- to twenty-two-year-olds go off to party, they go to learn how to become the leaders of our nation's military. Jeff Monkin, the head football coach of the army football team, said in an interview before the 2021 Army-Navy game that the most important line of his contract is this: to educate, train, and inspire future leaders. In my opinion, that should be at the heart of every teacher and coach in the country. This is what walking with Jesus does for us. As we walk with Jesus, we learn about him his grace and his glory. Walking with Jesus also trains us with how to handle the success and struggles of life on Earth. Lastly, the more we walk with Jesus, the more the Holy Spirit inspires and stirs our heart toward serving him. That is also part of being an asset for the Lord. To train, educate, and inspire other Christians.

Just like our basic training example, recruits don't show and train themselves. No, they have instructors who have been through it and know what it is supposed to look like. As we grow with Jesus, we educate, train, and inspire others for him. This is fulfilling the greatest mission ever given: the great commission.

> Then Jesus came to them and said, "All
> authority in heaven and on earth has been
> given to me. Therefore go and make disciples

of all nations, baptizing them in the name of
the Father and of the Son and of the Holy
Spirit, and teaching them to obey everything
I have commanded you. And surely I am with
you always, to the very end of the age. (Matt.
28:18–20 NIV)

Look at it this way: we get to be a part of the biggest tier 1 rescue mission in the history of the world. Without Jesus, people are bound and held captive by sin. Without rescue, they will surely die. If they die in their sin, they are lost forever. The ransom demanded is death. Understand we are not innocent. We bound ourselves. Lucky God did not leave us in bondage. God's love for us is the epitome of "no man left behind"; Jesus shows that when he paid that price on cavalry. By taking on our sin and shame by way of the cross, the ransom was paid in full. Our mission is not to go take out the bad guy. Our mission is to go tell people that the enemy has been defeated, and they no longer have to live in the bondage of sin!

Understand you are called to be an asset for the Lord, for your family, friends, coworkers, neighbors, and strangers. I know that can seem overwhelming. Remember, however, this is a process. We all must go through the pipeline. This process starts with the basics. It does not matter how long we have been a Christian, all of us can benefit by going back to the basics. Here are some questions to ask yourself: How are your quiet times with God? How is your church attendance? How is your giving? How is your prayer life? All of these answers can be tough to hear. If you're like me, the answer to some or all of these questions may sting a little bit. If they do, that's okay, but they don't have to sting forever. We can always go back to boot camp. Just like when college athletes return from break, strength coaches take time to reteach the basics. I remember an interview ESPN did with Nick Saban, the head football coach at the University of Alabama, where he talked about how the first few practices of bowl prep were always to reteach the basics. This is something we as Christians could benefit from. Take however long you need—two weeks, four weeks, or like real basic training nine to ten weeks—and focus on the basics. Your prayer life, your time with God, your time worshiping him with others (church), and finally, your status in the great commission. God will use that time of focusing on the basics to strengthen your faith!

Now you may be thinking that there is no way God could create anything out of me, especially someone he can depend on. My life is messed up. My past is too bad. I am too far gone. Or maybe the saddest of all, you may be saying I wish I could but I missed my chance for the Lord. Friend, I want to encourage you today! If you still have breath in your lungs, God has a plan for you. Even when you think all you are is just some old bones, God can turn what man sees as useless into useful.

Let's look at this in scripture.

> The hand of the Lord was on me, and he brought me out by the Spirit of the Lord and set me in the middle of a valley; it was full of bones. He led me back and forth among them, and I saw a great many bones on the floor of the valley, bones that were very dry. He asked me, "Son of man, can these bones live?"
>
> I said, "Sovereign Lord, you alone know."
>
> Then he said to me, "Prophesy to these bones and say to them, 'Dry bones, hear the word of the Lord! This is what the Sovereign Lord says to these bones: I will make breath enter you, and you will come to life. I will

attach tendons to you and make flesh come upon you and cover you with skin; I will put breath in you, and you will come to life. Then you will know that I am the Lord.'"

So I prophesied as I was commanded. And as I was prophesying, there was a noise, a rattling sound, and the bones came together, bone to bone. I looked, and tendons and flesh appeared on them and skin covered them, but there was no breath in them.

Then he said to me, "Prophesy to the breath; prophesy, son of man, and say to it, 'This is what the Sovereign Lord says: Come, breath, from the four winds and breathe into these slain, that they may live.'" So I prophesied as he commanded me, and breath entered them; they came to life and stood up on their feet—a vast army.

Then he said to me: "Son of man, these bones are the people of Israel. They say, 'Our bones are dried up and our hope is gone; we are cut off.' Therefore prophesy and say to them: 'This is what the Sovereign Lord says: My people, I am going to open your graves and bring you up from them; I will bring you back to the land of Israel. Then you, my people, will know that I am the Lord, when I open your graves and bring you up from them. I will put my Spirit in you and you will live, and I will settle you in your own land. Then you will know that I the Lord have spoken, and I have done it, declares the Lord.'" (Ezek. 37:1–14)

We see in the scriptures that what man thinks is a waste, God turned into a mighty asset for himself! So let this be an encouragement to you. You are not too far gone. Your past is not too bad, and it does not have to define your future. You may feel like you are living in a grave, but remember, we love, worship, and serve the God who conquered the grave! He's the only one who can call you out of it, and right now, he is calling your name. So today we need to listen: to hear with open ears and open hearts the rattle of what God is going to do in our lives. Believe that he is able and trust that he will! We also need to be open to let God tear down the things in our life that don't belong. He will strip us down to dry bones and build us back up for his glory and renown.

I want to be transparent in our journey together. With that being said, there is something you need to know about me. I am a nerd at heart. I love superhero movies, video games, and Harry Potter. When I was thinking of an example to tie a bow in this chapter, my mind went back to one of the Harry Potter movies. In the scene, Harry and his friends are training to fight the villain Voldemort. Harry tells all of his friends that every great wizard started right where they are. In school and learning the basics. The same is true for us. Every great man or woman of God each started at the same place, the basics. This is so important to understand because as humans we love to compare ourselves to others. If you compare yourself to great men and women of faith in your life, you will never measure up. This can create a sense of being overwhelmed. When that happens, we are more likely to throw in the towel. Remember how you eat an elephant…one bite at a time. The same is true for us. Our journey with Jesus is day by day. If we get 1 percent closer to God every day in a week, month, or year, the change to your heart and life will be amazing! It is also no one else's journey. Everyone is unique and different. So everyone's purpose that God created each for will look different, even though we all have the same objective—to know God and make him known to the world.

I hope and pray that as we take this journey down the pipeline, that the lessons will help educate, train, and inspire your faith. Remember, God has a plan and purpose for your life. You can't get to the destination without starting at step 1.

> For, "Everyone who calls on the name of the Lord will be saved."
>
> How, then, can they call on the one they have not believed in? And how can they believe in the one of whom they have not heard? And how can they hear without someone preaching to them? And how can anyone preach unless they are sent? As it is written: "How beautiful are the feet of those who bring good news!" (Rom. 10:13–15)

2

Stay in Your Three-Foot World

You will keep in perfect peace
those whose minds are steadfast,
because they trust in you.

—Isaiah 26:3 (NIV)

In Mark Owens book, *No Hero: The Evolution of a Navy Seal*, he explains a lesson he learned while going through rock climbing training in Nevada. Now if you have never read that book, I want to encourage you to check it out. Mark explains in the book that he had a fear of heights, so this training was no walk in the park. While climbing a rock face in the desert he looked down and froze. Losing focus on his hand and footholds and letting fear creep in. The instructor swings down to give Mark some helpful advice.

"Hey, man," he said in a lazy, raspy voice. "Just stay in your three-foot world."

I was a couple of hundred feet up on the rock face, and I could barely think, let alone decipher his cryptic advice.

"What the hell are you talking about, bro?"

"Only focus on your three-foot world," he said. "Focus on what you can affect. You keep looking around and none of that——can help you right now, can it?"

I shook my head no.

"You're calculating how far you're going to fall," the instructor said. "You're looking down at Jeff, but he's not going to come up here and help. You're looking out at the strip. What are you going to do, gamble your way to the top? Don't look at me, I am not going to help you either. This is up to you. You're climbing this rock. Stay in your three-foot world"]

Fear will attack you at some point in life. It is important for us to know that even the baddest dudes on the planet (SEALS, Rangers, PJs, Marine Recon, Green Berets, SAS) get scared and freeze. No one likes to admit that, because we all have an issue with weakness. If we admit weakness, we admit we're not perfect. Now there's a sermon you can preach about that message, but we will continue to move forward. The first step is always admitting there is a problem. So what areas in your life are you letting fear creep in? Where have you let worry sink its claws in your life? Take a second before moving forward to ask God to show you, and help you overcome it.

Fear and worry are tools the enemy uses to ambush and attack us. To keep us from pressing forward in the gospel mission of Jesus. Where you find one you will always find the other. They work together like the old-school tag teams of the WWE. The Dudley Boyz, Legion of Doom, Road Warriors, Brothers of Destruction, all teams that knew how to work with each other, and were good at it. Fear and worry behave the same way. They know how to use each other to team up to defeat us. The enemy wants you in a state of fear and worry. It's hard to function with the mental and physical side effects of fear and worry. Understanding this, and taking the lesson of staying in our three-foot world can help us overcome our battle. Above anything else remember you are not in it alone. Jesus is always with you, going before you and fighting your battles! Don't forget he is undefeated!

So how does staying in your three-foot world teach us to overcome fear and worry? You might be thinking, "I can promise I am never going rock climbing, so I am good." The truth is every single person deals with these issues on a daily basis. It may be the fear of losing a job then worrying how you will provide for your family. Or the fear of not being enough and worrying your wife or husband will find someone else. The fear of failure and the worry of what everyone will think of you, or how they will see you if you fail. Fear of a medical diagnosis, and the worry of how you will beat it. All examples of how no matter what season of life you are in, you can easily find yourself frozen on a rock face.

When any or all of these situations happen in our life, it is easy to get frozen on the rock. No matter how much we try to remind ourselves of Bobby McFerrin's wisdom (don't worry, be happy now) the fear and worry still come. Remember you are not alone in this. Everyone has to deal with these emotions. In our example from Mark Owen, he was looking for help from anywhere. The world teaches us to do the same thing. When life gets tough, we look for a way out. This is why many people are struggling with substance abuse issues. Everyone knows that the drugs or alcohol don't make the problem go away, they just make you forget for a little while. The same is true with food. We run to the pantry to fill our stomach hoping this will take the place of the problem. That is why it's called comfort food. That sounds great, but eventually when the high wears off or you get hungry again and you realize you are still in the same place "frozen on the rock."

Also, we can be told worldly wisdom that may help for a moment, but then puts us back in the same place. Like someone will tell you just "let it go." Now if you're like me and have been told that you probably rolled your eyes at that person. Or maybe you were nice, but in your head, you say something like this: "Sure I'll just let it go! Do you think my name is Elsa? Do I look like I am living in an ice castle?" (I have two daughters so I have seen Frozen once or twice.) No, we can't just hope our problems will go away. The difference between being an asset or a liability is assets work the problem. Let me give you a personal example.

God helped show me this truth personally in 2021. When I say 2021 was a rough year, I may be underselling it. On January first my grandmother got to go home and be with Jesus. That's hard because we miss her, but I know she is doing so much better than we are. This is not the part of the story where I freeze, however, although the loss of a family member can cause fear. If you are going through that, you do not have to stay frozen in that moment or season of loss. When I froze was when my wife (who was not even thirty years old at the time) was diagnosed with thyroid cancer. If you are going to have cancer, they say that's the good kind to have because of how treatable it is. None of that information helped with my fear. A few weeks later after my grandmother passed, Gena was in surgery to remove her thyroid. We are blessed because they found it early because the cancer was very aggressive and because of that there were complications. They had to remove part of her vocal chord because the thyroid had grown into it. Also, the thyroid was pressing on her trachea so they were worried the cancer cells could have spread to other parts of her throat and other parts of her body. All of this is being told to me over the phone because hospitals were not allowing visitors (thanks, COVID). So there I was sitting in a parking garage of the hospital trying to figure out if my wife would be okay. Would she ever be able to talk again? Has the cancer spread? So I checked all the boxes of fear and worry that day. I may not have been hundreds of feet off the ground, but I was frozen in that moment. God did show his grace to me that day, though, when I got to FaceTime Gena and hear her voice (as weak as it was).

I lived in that state of fear and worry for a week until we went back for her post op appointment. The doctor told us they were sending us to UAB (biggest hospital in Alabama) to a team of specialists. The doctors at UAB were great. They recommended radiation therapy. They wanted to make sure whatever cancer cells were left would be nuked. The hard part of this was that my wife had to stay away from our kids (four and one) for about two weeks. Every bath time, getting to daycare, making lunches was all on my shoulders. We survived that (with help from our family) and went back in March for scans and everything looked good. We could finally take a breath or so I thought. While this had been going on with Gena, we were also dealing with some concerns with my oldest daughter. The day after we got that report that Gena's scans were good, my oldest daughter was diagnosed with autism. We knew something was going on with her because she had a speech delay. While other kids in her daycare class were putting words and phrases together, she was not. We took her to get tested to see what was wrong and how to help her. Autism was the diagnosis we got. The doctor asked if we had any questions. I had a million, but did not know where to start. A new set of worries crept into my heart. What would her life look like? I was worried about the hard things that she was going to have to face. When it's your kid having problems, it's hard. You see them around their peers and know they're falling behind in some areas. If you are like me, you blame yourself constantly. You not only let fear and worry in your life, you clear out a room for them to live with you. That's what I did. I went from the highest high to the lowest low in less than twenty-four hours.

Fear owned me for a while. I was its slave and it was my master. Out of all of that time there was a moment where God spoke this truth into my life. I remember being in the car with Gena after the first doctor's appointment where they told us she had cancer. In that moment where there were more questions than answers, fear consumed me and I just broke down. I could not look at her 'cause the tears were just flowing down my face. Every bad thought you could have was running through my mind. Above anything else I did not want to lose my best friend. I was frozen and could not function! Only by the grace of God was I able to focus on this one thought… Right now, it's not about me. So I took a deep breath and said a prayer (God, help me be strong for her). At that moment God took me back to Mark Owen's book. I could feel God speaking to me through the Holy Spirit: "Drew, stay in your three-foot world. Control what you can control and *trust me*."

I knew I had to get over the fear. I could not function in that space, at least not how my family needed me to function. When the fear overtook me, I was no longer an asset in my family I was a liability. So I tried to live the maxim of staying in my three-foot world. I approached both situations with that mindset. What can I do to help? What was in my control became my focus. It was never something huge. It was always a basic thing that needed to be done. When I was at school, loving my students and teaching with energy and passion on a daily basis was inside my three-foot world. Preparing a sermon to proclaim the gospel on a Wednesday night or Sunday morning was inside my three-foot world. Most times, it was just being present with my wife and kids. Making lunch for them or watching *Bluey* or *Toy Story*. All of it was inside my three-foot world. For Gena, it was just being a friend. Making sure I was always there to hug her when she needed it, or just be her person. I could not change the situation or make it go away; however, I could make the moment better. I wish I could say I was the model of what a husband and dad should be, but I know I let them down over this journey. It always seemed to happen when I let my focus go outside my three-foot world. Whenever I started to drift, I would remind myself to stay in my three-foot world.

Fear has negative effects on our physical and spiritual lives. Fear can weaken our immune system. When paired with worry, it can cause cardiovascular damage, and ulcers and decreased fertility are some of side effects that can occur. Also increased blood pressure, and an accelerated aging process. All of those are bad but the effects on our spiritual life are far worse. You were made to be in a relationship with God. It is an open and honest relationship. We don't have to pretend with God because he knows our heart. When we are worried and scared, he knows! We should never put on a front when we come before the throne. Fear and worry can bind you up. Remember our savior is the bondage breaker. Hebrews 4:16 tells us, "Let us then with confidence draw near to the throne of grace, that we may receive mercy and find grace to help in time of need" (ESV). God tells us to come confidently to him. It's hard to do that when you are bound with fear. The devil wants to keep you in that state of bondage. Remember his ultimate goal is to keep you as far away from God as possible.

As Christians, the three-foot world mindset can help us in our times of fear and worry. Will our faith shine its light in the darkness of fear? By the way, be prepared because it always hits you the hardest when it's dark or when you're alone. It seems like in the dark is where the bad things live, and where the bad things want to fight. So will we run and hide when the lights get low, or will we trust God and draw near to him? These are real questions that you will have to answer in your life. Maybe you are in that dark place today. God is calling you to stand up and fight. I want to share some good news with you today, though.

You are not in the valley alone. In this Christian life Jesus is our tag team partner. He is the greatest of all time (GOAT), and he is undefeated. So trust in Jesus.

Trust is our weapon to combat fear and worry. They make us doubt, and doubt does not draw you near to God. It drives you the opposite way like you have an Acme rocket strapped to your back while wearing roller skates. We prove this to be true when we ask questions: "How can a good God let this happen to me?" or simply "Where is God?" These are reasonable questions and it's okay to ask them. The issue is where do we run to for answers. Do we run to the world, or do we run to God? The world teaches us to blame God. God, however, teaches us something different. God sees us as children so come to him like a father! Whether you had a good father or no father in your life. God is our perfect heavenly father, always inviting us in no matter what is going on in our life. He is always ready for our questions. Most importantly, He is always walking with us when we don't understand.

A parent never wants his or her kid to hurt. I know this because when they told us the diagnosis about my daughter my heart sank to the floor. I was so worried about problems she was going to have to face. I never want her to have to feel any hurt or pain if I can help it. The hardest part was I knew I could not help. No matter what comes her way I know I will always be there to love her when she is happy and when she is hurting. God is the same way with us. He loves us like sons and daughters. He is with you to celebrate the good, and embrace you in the bad; to love you on the mountain top and in the valley.

In the book of Isaiah, we see this truth over and over again. I would like to show you two examples of who God is so that you can lean on these truths in times of worry and fear. The first is Isaiah 26:3: "You will keep him in perfect peace whose mind stayed on you, because he trusts in you" (ESV). Fear and worry can keep you in constant tension. That tension can cause us to lose rest and sleep. The loss of rest/sleep can add other physical problems on top of the ones caused by worry and fear. They can also hinder our spiritual life too. When we are exhausted is when the devil wants to come to us with his lies. We see this example in the life of Jesus when he is tempted in the desert. God, however, does not want us to live like this. God wants to keep us not just in peace but in perfect peace. Perfect peace can only be found in God. This is how Jesus overcame the devil in the desert. He relied on and trusted God to fulfill him instead of the temptations that the devil offered.

How is that possible? Once again easy to say, hard to do. Lucky for us we can find the answer in the Bible (hopefully, you are starting to see a theme). Psalm 23 tells us that even though I walk through the valley of the shadow of death I won't be afraid because God is with me. Not only is he with me but he comforts me, and he leads me to peace! We find ourselves in the darkest valleys of life when fear and worry attack us. Sitting on the beach in the summer is not their battleground. It's when life gets cold and dark. Remember that's where the bad things live, and that's where the bad things fight. We don't have a God who lets us walk in the valley alone. No, God is with us always. In the coldest, darkest, scariest moments of our life he is standing right beside us. Not only is he with you, he goes before you (Deut. 31:8 and Isa. 52:12), leading us to peace and rest. This only happens if we trust him.

Let's take a minute to look over Isaiah 40:25–31 to see what happens when we put our hope and trust in the Lord in our hardest moments:

> "To whom will you compare me?
> Or who is my equal?" says the Holy One.
> Lift up your eyes and look to the heavens:

Who created all these?
He who brings out the starry host one by one
and calls forth each of them by name.
Because of his great power and mighty
strength,
not one of them is missing.
Why do you complain, Jacob?
Why do you say, Israel,
"My way is hidden from the Lord;
my cause is disregarded by my God"?
Do you not know?
Have you not heard?
The Lord is the everlasting God,
the Creator of the ends of the earth.
He will not grow tired or weary,
and his understanding no one can fathom.
He gives strength to the weary
and increases the power of the weak.
Even youths grow tired and weary,
and young men stumble and fall;
but those who hope in the Lord
will renew their strength.
They will soar on wings like eagles;
they will run and not grow weary,
they will walk and not be faint.

Let this Word of God pour into your heart! First, there is
no one who is equal to our God. We don't even have anything
to compare him to. So when we say that God is with us, we are
saying we have the best with us! Not only is he on his own level
but he is the creator of everything. When things start breaking
down, it is always best to go to the creator to find out how to fix

it. So when life starts breaking down and getting sideways, run to God to learn how to put the pieces back together.

The second thing to take from this is that God sees you. Your problems are not hidden from him. Fear and worry have a way of making us think that no one sees or understands our pain. When this turns into thinking no one cares, you are getting off onto the on-ramp to a little place I like to call depression. We have a God who is the star breather and the universe maker. He is big enough to see every issue and know exactly what is going on. Knowing that we must ask ourselves this question: why would I ever look anywhere else for help or understanding?

The third and most important thing is that when we hope/trust in the Lord he (God) will renew our strength. When fear and worry cause you to freeze and you feel like you can't go on, put your trust in God and you will see your strength start to rise. It may not be like superman strength (although he can give us that), but it's enough strength to get past our hardest moments. Like just getting out of bed the next day after you got bad news. Making supper after a hard day at work. Just a few examples where we don't think we can go on, but God gets us to that next handhold on the rock.

The old adage in the military is, "Hope is not a strategy. The brave men of special operations never just "hope" the problem will work itself out. No, they trust their training, rely on good Intelligence, and believe in the community to get the job done. As followers of Jesus hope/trust is not a strategy we turn to when everything else fails. It's our battle plan, and there is no option B! Why should we do this? First, he is the one who will never let us down. Second God is always up, always working, and never gets tired. Third, we trust God because he is a man of his word. So if he says he will stand beside you, He will! Paul tells us this in 2 Timothy 4:17, "But the Lord stood by me and strengthened me, so that through me the message might be fully proclaimed and all the Gentiles might hear it. So I was rescued from the lion's mouth" (ESV). Not only will he stand by you, he will also rescue you. That means God has your best interest at heart! He wants to lead you to perfect peace. Even when the world is spinning out of control, God is holding onto you!

All of these things are attributes of God's unwavering character. Even when we let him down he is still faithful to us. So it is in him we place our trust. Even when we can't see the entire picture or the next step, we hope and trust that God will bring us to safety. That is the only way I was able to make it through the situation I was in. I stayed in my three-foot world. Controlling what I could knowing that God wanted my focus there. Even when there was a big doctor's appointment coming up I controlled the controllable. Making breakfast, getting the girls ready for daycare, picking them up, making sure we made all our appointments were all examples of things I could control. That is what God is calling each of us to do. Handle the things he puts in front of us and trust him to take care of the things we can't. No matter how much I worried I could not control what the doctor was going to say about my wife or my daughter. More importantly, I had zero control over what a test result was going to be, or when they would be in. Waiting on medical test results will make anyone go crazy. What I did have control over was right in front of my face. Loving my wife and kids. They needed me to be an example of how God loves us.

I am not saying this to brag about myself. I bring that up to give a real-world example of what sticking to this maxim looks like. When I stayed in my three-foot world, I became an asset that my family could depend on. I also learned with every challenge, setback, and victory God can be counted on. In every step, twist, and turn of this journey he has been with me, always protecting and leading me to his perfect peace. Even when I started to panic or freak out, God was always there to be my calm in the chaos.

If you struggle with fear and worry, spend some time with Jesus today. Open the Bible, get down on your knees and talk to your heavenly father. He loves you and cares about you and what you are going through. You were not meant to stay frozen on the rock. Check out the following Bible verses on trust and worry.

Hebrews 13:6, Isaiah 43:1–3, Psalm 46:10, Psalm 56:3, Psalm 121:1–2, Romans 8:31.

Trust God and stay in your three-foot world!

3

Quiet Professionals

May I never boast except in the cross of our
Lord Jesus Christ, through which the world has
been crucified to me, and I to the world.

—Galatians 6:14

Special Operations Forces (SOF) are elite military units. They are highly trained in a vast array of fighting techniques on land, sea, and air. They also learn different languages, how to pick locks, even evasive driving techniques. Becoming proficient in all the skills they might need to carry out the operations of the United States Military at a high level. The resumes of these operators set them apart from not only the general public, but also the rest of the military community.

In this elite community is a group with a decorated past and proud heritage. If you say Special Forces (SF), then you are talking about them. The United States Army's Green Berets name comes from the headgear that they wear as part of their uniform. This group was not officially recognized till nearly a decade after its formation when president John F Kennedy wrote about them in a presidential memo. Like the trident of the Navy Seals, the green beret is a badge of honor. It is an outward symbol of distinction to the world that the individual wearing it is part of the best of the best. The beret does not make the soldier wearing it elite. It does, however, encompass the legacy that has been laid by the soldiers who came before them, and ones who will come after them. They are always doing their part to uphold the proud tradition of the Army Green Berets.

Although The Green Berets started in 1952 as part of the US Army Psychological Warfare Division, the roots of this elite force can be traced all the way back to World War II. Its purpose was to create a force that excels in unconventional warfare. Since its creation the Green Berets focus on five primary missions: unconventional warfare, counterinsurgency, direct action mission, reconnaissance, and foreign internal defense. Each member of the Green Berets has to come from the pipeline. The pipeline is the journey of each soldier from basic training, through selection and the Q course all the way to graduation day.

The United States Army Special Forces is a community of brotherhood. While they rely on everyone in the community for mission success, each SF unit is self-sustaining. All members can serve multiple roles; whatever their MOS (Military Occupational Specialty) and being a rifleman. Basically, that means each member of the SOF community can be an asset in the fight. Always ready to put down whatever they are doing at the time and pick up their weapon and engage in the fight. Each twelve-man team is able to operate in remote locations for long periods of time. Because of the knowledge of different languages, and the unique skill set of its members, SF units can be successful in completing their mission in any part of the world.

Even with all these skills, SF personnel take on the title of the "quiet professional." This mantra is wired into the DNA of every green beret, because of the nature of their work being mostly secret. So most missions carried out by this group of elite soldiers are rarely made known to the public. They are called upon to work behind enemy lines, to train gorilla forces, and sometimes work as diplomats. Only so often in the news or in movies do we learn the heroic stories of these elite soldiers.

Keeping the activities of life classified is something that the average Joe is not able to do on a daily basis. In a world where everyone has a social platform to display their life and accomplishments, the green berets do the opposite. This is crazy because if we're honest these heroes have more to brag about than the vast majority of the country. First only a small percentage of the military make it through the selection process, but it does not end there. Being a part of that community is something you work to earn every single day. These soldiers are always working, striving, and training to be at an elite level for whenever the country calls upon the use of their unique and elite skills. Some of that training is really cool. Like HALO jumps (high altitude, low opening), jungle training, and arctic training. I read an article on arctic training. Basically, they go up north in the winter and jump in the water. Then they practice getting out of the ice on their own. Then they practice how to warm up and survive. So I might have been underselling it when I said they do some cool stuff. All the videos we post of our pets, complaints about the teenagers working at the fast-food restaurant we like to go to, or just using Facebook as a therapy session. It is not in the same ballpark with what these brave men accomplish. They walk the road of humility, while the rest of us are thrust toward total self-absorption. We think we have to present ourselves like a baller or a shot caller (bonus points if you get the song reference).

Pride is one weapon that the devil uses to bring you down. So often we use all of our skills and accomplishments to build ourselves up. Gladly puffing out our chest and screaming to the world to look at me. Look at all that I have done, and look at all I have. With that comes a world of problems. Remember the old saying pride comes before the fall is 100 percent true. When we don't get the recognition we feel we deserve, we can become jaded toward our families, friends, and more importantly, our faith. Understand when we take on this attitude and remove ourselves from loving our friends and family, and serving in our church, the enemy wins. Remember he (the devil) wants to do whatever he can to keep you from working for God and loving others.

This is something I have struggled with my entire life. Always trying to live a life God would be proud of. As I look back, though, the times that got me in trouble were when my life was all about me. My focus was on my glory and success and not God's. I can't count the times I have gotten my feelings hurt or all the wasted time pouting because my focus was all on me. If I did not get the credit I thought I deserved, or the attention I felt I should have, my reaction was not Christ-like. Basically, I sullied up and got all up in my feels. It's only natural to want that pat on the back. The "atta boy" for the work you do. This is why we have a society that is consumed with how many views, likes, and mentions we get. Pride has a way of taking the work we do that starts pure, but ends up being more about glorifying ourselves rather than glorifying God. Pride is a master at blowing us up and shrinking God down.

This struggle with pride is what Paul is discussing in his letter to the Galatians. The Christians in Galatia were struggling with the act of circumcision. Some were preaching that to be a follower of Jesus you had to be circumcised. They struggled with where Old Testament theology fits into with faith in Jesus. These people were focused on what they did in the flesh. They took pride in the outward. Thinking that the outward somehow had influence on salvation. If we are not careful, we can fall into this trap just like them. This is why Paul, through guidance of the Holy Spirit, writes in Galatians 6:14, "May I never boast except in the cross of our Lord Jesus Christ, through which the world has been crucified to me, and I to the world." This is the definition of the biblical quiet professional. It is never about what I do or have done, but all about what Jesus did and is going to do! Remember the call of Jesus is to take up your cross (die to the wants, needs, and desires of this world), and follow him. That means to die to the wants, needs, desires of this world, and live for Jesus.

As Christians, it is for our benefit that we adopt the mind-set of the Green Berets and become quiet professionals. In the journey toward becoming a tier 1 asset (better disciple), we will face schemes from the enemy to take us out of the fight. Knowing the enemy and having intel on his tactics is crucial to give yourself the best chance to be successful in the battle. Pride is one of those tactics the devil will use against you. The enemy does not play with the same rules as us. In John (10:10), Jesus tells us that the enemy comes to kill, steal, and destroy. So know the devil does not have your best interest at heart. He wants to kill your hope, steal your joy, and destroy the foundation of your faith. He is the ultimate terrorist!

What you boast about is what you are proud of. When we have a deep personal investment in things, we want to tell the world about them. Whether it be our children, or our career, our possessions, or even our role in the church. The subject of what we boast about does not matter in the context we are discussing. The issue is the alignment of our heart. No matter what our kids do, or the accomplishments of our career, or how great of an athlete we were in high school. (Everyone has an Al Bundy friend. You know the one who scored four touchdowns in a single game at Polk High School. Waiting at a moment's notice to tell the story of the glory years.) Although all of these things are great and are blessings from God, none of them are even comparable to the life and work of Jesus Christ. Think about it, even if you scored four touchdowns in a single game, made a million dollars, or even discovered the cure for cancer, none of it would ever be enough to bridge the gap that sin created between us and God.

Understanding this truth helps us line up our hearts with God's heart. We must hold on to Romans 3:23: "For all have sinned and fallen short of the glory of God" (NIV). No matter our greatest deeds our sin has separated us from a holy God. Our bad far outweighs our good, and we can never balance that scale. We are unworthy of any love and grace from God. Because of this we stand condemned on our own. However, where our sin was great, God's love is far greater. Romans 5:8 beautifully describes this relationship. "But God shows his love for us in that while we were still sinners, Christ died for us" (ESV). We have a God who loves us so much that he stepped off the throne in heaven, and came to Earth taking on flesh and giving his life as the ultimate sacrifice. By doing so he satisfied the wages of sin. Knowing this, how could we ever boast about anything but Jesus?

I want you to understand that taking on this mindset is hard. Like really hard to do. It's easy to say, but extremely complicated to execute on a daily basis. Remember Jesus never said it would be easy. One reason this is hard is because we often forget who is at the center of the universe. It is easy to get lost in focusing on our little part of this planet, while forgetting that our lives are being played out in the theater called the cosmos. Our little galaxy is not even the center of the universe. So when we think the world revolves around us, we are not just wrong; we are universally wrong. We are blessed, however, with God's Word to remind us who is the star of the show. Genesis 1:1 makes this real clear: "In the beginning, God created the heavens and the earth" (ESV). So from the beginning, it has never been about us. It has always been about God, and his glory, and his renown.

Isaiah 26:8 says this:

> Yes, Lord, walking in the way of your
laws,
> we wait for you;
> your name and renown
> are the desire of our hearts. (NIV)

So the question we must ask ourselves is this; who is one the throne of our life. Whoever sits on the throne of our life is who we try to glorify. If Jesus is king of your life, then this statement by Isaiah should be written in the center of our heart. If you have a life mission statement without something like Isaiah 26:8 in it, then you are missing the point. How do we kill pride? We do it by taking the spotlight off us and shining it on Jesus, by living a life where the desire of our heart is to know God and make him known to a lost and dying world. If we do that, there is a reward for us. Paul shares with Timothy this exact encouragement of living a life for the glory of God when he tells him in chapter 4 of his second letter that he (Paul) fought the good fight and kept the faith, and because of that there is a crown of righteousness waiting on him in heaven. The same goes with us: keep fighting the good fight, keep running the race, and keep the faith because we will be with Jesus again one day. Hearing Jesus say well done should be what our heart longs for.

The battle of pride is one we must fight every day. We fool ourselves if we think that this is a one and done battle. No, the battle of pride is like a college football rivalry. I see this every day with where I live (the great state of Alabama). The Alabama and Auburn rivalry is never ending. Although they play only once a year, the members of each side are ready to fight that battle (majority of the time with words, but sometimes with physical altercations) 24 hours a day and 365 days a year. This is why Jesus gives us instruction to die to yourself daily. Luke 9:23 records this charge from Jesus, "Then he said to them all: Whoever wants to be my disciple must deny themselves and take up their cross daily and follow me" (NIV). To be victorious over pride we must prepare to fight it every day. If you give the enemy an inch in your heart, he will take a mile. So be prepared for the altercation daily and remember Jesus is always watching your six o'clock.

Also, rely on your community. If you don't have a solid group of Christians in your life who will be honest with you, then I encourage you to ask God to connect you with a group like that. If your "friends" only tell you that you're right all the time and never call you on your screwups, then they are not really your friends. Remember, you will become what you surround yourself with. So keep your circle tight with people who are after God's heart and not the world's glory.

Now don't get this confused; the call to be a quiet professional is not a charge to never speak about how great God is and how much the world needs him. Quiet is not silent. No, Jesus told us to go tell the world about him (Matt. 28:18–20). By taking on the quiet professional mindset we can become an asset equipped to carry out this mission. Always working, always studying, growing deeper in our relationship with God is what every Christian should strive for. Dying to pride every day and living for the *glory* of God by the *grace* of God. Jesus is always worth boasting about.

If you struggle with pride, take some time and talk to God about it. Remember he is not scared of your problems. Also check out the following verses about pride: Jeremiah 9:23–24, 1 John 2:16, Mark 7:20–23, Proverbs 18:10–12, Proverbs 15:25–33.

Let your work be done in the shadow of the spotlight that is fixed on Jesus.

$$4$$

"Murph" Part 1

And Jesus said, "Father, forgive them, for they know not what they do." And they cast lots to divide his garments.

—Luke 23:34

The book that sparked my interest in special operations is *Lone Survivor* by Marcus Luttrell. It is about his firsthand account of Operation Red Wings that took place in Afghanistan in 2005. If you have not read it, I encourage you to make time to read it. Marcus's story about the heroism his friends and teammates showed on a mountain side across the world will captivate your heart. If you are not a big reader (thank you for reading my book by the way), there is a great movie based on this book as well. Operation Red Wings at the time was the largest loss of special operation members at one time since the beginning of Operation Enduring Freedom. The names of each of the brave men who gave the ultimate sacrifice can be found at the end of this chapter.

In the book, we are introduced to four American heroes: Gunner's Mate Second Class Danny Dietz; Sonar Technician

Second Class Matthew Axelson, Hospital Corpsman Second Class Marcus Luttrell, and Lt. Michael Murphy. Each of these brave men earned the title of Navy Seal. Their mission was to scout a known terrorist, Amhad Shah. The mission started with a night insertion of the four-man team. After a few false insertions to throw off any enemy watching, the team began its hike to the overlook position. The objective was to locate the HVT (high-value target), the call for the QRF (Quick Reaction Force) to link up with the four-man SEAL team and capture or Kill Amhad Shah. The mission, however, was compromised when the four-man team was spotted by locals, and then the locals reported them to the Taliban. This led to a fierce firefight. Marcus and his team mates were outnumbered and in a bad tactical position. The Taliban held the high ground. For our journey together we will look at the actions of one of the members of the team during these intense moments, Lt. Michael Murphy or Murph as his friends knew him.

Although any SEAL is always ready to lead and be led, it was Lt. Murphy who was the OIC (officer in command) of this mission. Matthew Axelson was the point man and lead sniper. Danny Dietz was in charge of communications. Marcus Luttrell was the medic and back up sniper. I want to draw two big connections while looking at the heroic action of Lt. Murphy and his brothers on the mountain that day. The first is what true character under fire looks like, and how that can impact our faith.

Before we get to the events of Operation Red Wings, I want to do my best to introduce you to Lt. Michael Murphy. He grew up in Patchogue, New York. As a kid you could find him playing sports and serving as a lifeguard at the local lake. After graduating from Penn State, he was accepted to a few law schools, but he decided he wanted to become a Navy SEAL. The Medal of Honor website bio said he did a mentoring program at the US Merchant Marine College at Kings Point New York.

After graduation from BUDS (Basic Underwater Demolition/ SEAL training) and earning his trident, he linked up with SDV Team 1. The teams took him all over the world, from different countries in the middle east, to parts of Africa. He was awarded the Medal of Honor for his actions in Operation Red Wings. He Also received the following medals and awards during his career: Purple Heart, Combat Action Ribbon, the Joint Service Commendation Medal, the Navy and Marine Corps Commendation Medal, Afghanistan Campaign Ribbon, and National Defense Service Medal. (For more about the life and career of Lt. Michael Murphy, check out his page on the Navy's Medal of Honor website as well as the Lt. Michael Murphy Navy Seal Museum.)

In Afghanistan with SDVT 1 as an assistant officer with Alpha platoon is where the action of Murphy and his team are recorded in Marcus Luttrell's book. That is where we will pick up the story today. The four-man SEAL team was pinned down on all sides by enemy fighters. Navy Seals pride themselves on being some of the best marksmen in the world; however, when you don't hold the high ground in the fight, you are at a tactile disadvantage. (As a side lesson in your life and Christian journey, always try to hold the high ground.) Not only were they taking small arms fire but they were also getting mortars and RPGs (rocket-propelled grenade) lobbed in on top of them. Each member of the team was now injured and in real trouble. After falling back (literally falling off the mountain) Lt. Murphy with no regard for himself left cover to try to make a phone call on the sat phone. Until this point, the rest of the members of their team back at the airbase had no idea the trouble they were in because of communication issues. Communication is key in all areas of life. Lt. Murphy knew without communication back to his support he and his team were doomed. Lt. Murphy left his cover from the enemy fire and went out fully exposed to call for help. While being fired upon by the enemy Lt. Murphy calmly relayed his team's position to the command. Even while taking a round to the back during the call Lt. Murphy picked the receiver of the sat phone back up and finished the call with "Thank you." Lt. Murphy then returned to the fight. Even with the world burning all around him and literally taking fire from the enemy he still said, "Thank you" at the end of a phone call. That is a true example of character under fire!

It would be safe to say that Lt. Murphy's character was above reproach. Now I don't know about you, but I can't say I would do the same thing. I would like to think that I would; however, I can look back on times in my life when things were going wrong and my character was not something to be proud of. When work was hard, I would be a real jerk to my family. I let pressure cause me to have a short fuse with my wife and my friends. I even let internal stress cause external problems with my players, coworkers, and even myself. When something would not go my way, in my anger, I would scream every profanity I know. Now I never did this around people, but I say this to remind you your character is made up partly of what you do when no one is watching. None of my actions were examples of good biblical character.

As we go further, I want to explain to you what character is. A Google search will bring you to this definition: *the mental and moral qualities distinctive to an individual.* The Drew Hall definition is simply this; character is your outward actions reflecting the contents of your heart to the world. It's showing what you really believe in by the way you act and talk. Lt. Murphy is one of the greatest examples I have found for this definition; still using manners even while literally taking fire from the enemy.

You don't show your character when life is going well. You and I can always do the right thing when life is going our way.

The truth is you show your character when the world is burning all around you. Show me who you are under pressure, show me what you do when it's hard to do the right thing, and then you will show me your real character. Most of us lose our mind over small things. Having to wait in line at the drive through, the grocery store not having the items we want, or having to wear a mask in places. This plus many other situations are day to day examples where we show our character.

There are bigger situations than that, though. How do we act when we get fired from a job? Do you get angry and search for pity? How do you communicate with your spouse when you screw up? Do you blame him or her and point out mistakes? How do you respond when people let you down? Do those people become dead to you? Take a second and think, does my world look like the walking dead? Remember, you can't have a relationship with a zombie. What do you do when someone asks for help that can never repay you? Do you give willingly even if no one is watching? How we answer these questions with our actions, attitude, and words shows the world the inside of our heart.

As Christians, our character should be of the utmost importance to us. We should always have a sense of urgency to do the right thing. Not just when it's convenient, or when a lot of people are watching. Every moment we have breath in our lungs we should look to do the right thing. Once we take on the title of Jesus's follower, we represent more than ourselves. We represent the King of kings and the Lord of lords. In the coaching world, we explain it like this. Be more concerned with the name on the front of the jersey than the one on the back. Our character being above reproach is mission critical. If we are bad people, why would anyone want any part of Jesus?

We should strive to live this way because the Bible tells us to. In 2 Corinthians 5:20, it says, "Therefore, we are ambassadors for Christ, God making his appeal through us. We implore you on behalf of Christ, be reconciled to God" (ESV). Paul tells us that God is making his appeal to the world through us. What is his appeal you ask? It's simply this: I (God) love you, your sin has separated us, but I sent my son Jesus to pay your price, through him you are forgiven. That is the role we play in this amazing redemptive story of God's unfailing love. We get to show the world Jesus in us through our character and actions. We are entrusted with the greatest news ever, and called to show it to the world.

Now if you are like me, you need to see an example to understand how to do it—a demonstration of how to have godly character on a daily basis. Thankfully for us The Bible gives us clear examples of what Christian character under fire should and should not look like. The beauty of the Bible is we can see this example in the same passage of scripture.

Our first example of Christian character under fire needs to look no further than Jesus. The entirety of Jesus's life is an example of the character we should reflect in our life. However, for this example I want to look at Jesus's last few hours on this Earth. After being arrested in the garden the night before and tried and sentenced to death by way of the cross Jesus shows us what godly character under fire looks like. He was beaten and whipped to within an inch of his life. Made to carry through the streets the very thing that would kill him through the streets. He was taken and stripped naked and then nailed to a cross for all the world to see. It is this moment where Jesus shows us what real Christian character under fire looks like.

> When they came to the place called the Skull, they crucified him there, along with the criminals—one on his right, the other on his left. Jesus said, "Father, forgive them, for they do not know what they are doing." And they divided up his clothes by casting lots. The

people stood watching, and the rulers even
sneered at him. They said, "He saved others;
let him save himself if he is God's Messiah,
the Chosen One." (Luke 23:33–35 NIV)

So here we find Jesus in the hardest spot in his life, being mocked, and dying in a way reserved for the worst offenders. It was so bad that the Roman empire would not kill a Roman citizen by way of the cross. This was not an honorable way to die. That is where we find the son of God, though. Through all of it Jesus's character never cracked. With nails in his hands and feet he looks at the people and asks God to forgive them. This is crazy! When we feel like someone has done us wrong, we ask for God's strong arm of justice to swiftly come down upon their head. Jesus, who actually could call for justice to rain down, instead asks for forgiveness. We can see clearly what was in Jesus's heart by his actions and words on the hardest day of his life.

Now you may be thinking that is awesome. I am glad my savior has that kind of unbreakable character. But I am not Jesus. Last time I checked I never healed the blind, walked on water, turned water into wine, or raised the dead. I can't even read my Bible daily! So there is no way I can have that kind of character. That's 100 percent true! On our own we can't, but with God we can! Let's look at the character of one of Jesus's followers when he was under pressure. I think we can all relate to him.

Peter followed closely after Jesus was arrested. You have to understand there were some sketchy moments for Jesus followers. The disciples had no idea if they would be the ones arrested next. So the fear and pressure weighing on their heart was heavy. It is at this moment we see Peter's character. In Luke 22:54–62, it says,

Then they seized him and led him away,
bringing him into the high priest's house,

and Peter was following at a distance. And when they had kindled a fire in the middle of the courtyard and sat down together, Peter sat down among them. Then a servant girl, seeing him as he sat in the light and looking closely at him, said, "This man also was with him." But he denied it, saying, "Woman, I do not know him." And a little later someone else saw him and said, "You also are one of them." But Peter said, "Man, I am not." And after an interval of about an hour still another insisted, saying, "Certainly this man also was with him, for he too is a Galilean." But Peter said, "Man, I do not know what you are talking about." And immediately, while he was still speaking, the rooster crowed. And the Lord turned and looked at Peter. And Peter remembered the saying of the Lord, how he had said to him, "Before the rooster crows today, you will deny me three times." And he went out and wept bitterly. (NIV)

When the pressure became great, Peter denied knowing the Lord. How often does our character deny knowing Jesus? When we get put in a tough situation, do our words and actions say to the world, "I know Jesus"? If you are honest with yourself, be prepared because the answers can be hard to handle. When Peter realized what he had done, the Bible says he wept bitterly. Maybe you are in the same place, realizing you have royally screwed it up over and over again, letting your actions in hard moments deny Jesus, thinking, *Why should I even try?* Well, failure is never final unless you let failure be fatal. Just like Peter, our story does not end there.

In Acts, after Jesus has risen from the dead, and ascended into heaven we find Peter showing us godly character.

> Men of Israel, hear these words: Jesus of Nazareth, a man attested to you by God with mighty works and wonders and signs that God did through him in your midst, as you yourselves know—this Jesus, delivered up according to the definite plan and foreknowledge of God, you crucified and killed by the hands of lawless men. God raised him up, losing the pangs of death, because it was not possible for him to be held by it. (Acts 2:22–24 ESV)

So Peter goes from denying Jesus to claiming him as Messiah in front of all the people in Jerusalem. This happens because Peter's heart was different. Not from a self-help book or a TED talk, but from the Holy Spirit.

Just like Peter, our character is not based on our past actions. No matter how badly we want to, we can't change the past. We can, however, with the help of the Holy Spirit, do the next right thing. When the world starts burning and the pressure begins to mount, we can show the world Jesus through our actions and words. When you have a tough meeting at work, let your coworkers see Jesus in your temperament. When you're at a party with your friends, let them see Jesus in your actions. When you talk to your spouse or kids, let them hear Jesus in your words. Let your character speak Jesus so loudly to the world that it will never question if we are Christians.

To summarize, be an ambassador for Jesus with your character. Understanding failure is never final unless you let it be. Always remember you are not in the fire alone. God is with you always. He understands the struggle. When it gets hard, lean on his strength to do the right thing. I have heard Nick Saban use this quote in a lot of the talks he has given, and it has stuck with me ever since. Coach Saban says, "What you do speaks so loudly, I can't hear a word you say." That should be our goal in our walk with Jesus. What we do speaks Jesus so loudly; we don't have to tell people we are Jesus followers.

If your character has been falling short lately, spend some time with Jesus! Stop dwelling on past mistakes. Remember in Jesus we stand forgiven! That should be encouragement enough to want to live a life of godly character. Take some time and check out what God's Word says about character.

As in 1 Corinthians 15:33, Philippians 4:8, Proverbs 10:9, Psalm 25:21, Titus 2:7–8.

"Roger that sir, Thank you" (Lt. Michael Murphy).

The brave men who gave the ultimate sacrifice for our country and freedom:

Lt. (SEAL) Michael P. Murphy, Sonar Technician (Surface) Second Class (SEAL) Matthew G. Axelson, Gunner's Mate Second Class (SEAL) Danny P. Dietz, Machinist Mate Second Class (SEAL) Eric S. Patton, Senior Chief Information Systems Technician (SEAL) Daniel R. Healy, Quartermaster Second Class (SEAL) James Suh, Chief Fire Controlman (SEAL) Jacques J. Fontan, Lt. Cmdr. (SEAL) Erik S. Kristensen, Electronics Technician First Class (SEAL) Jeffery A. Lucas, Lt. (SEAL) Michael M. McGreevy Jr., Hospital Corpsman First Class (SEAL) Jeffrey S. Taylor, Staff Sgt. Shamus O. Goare, Chief Warrant Officer Corey J. Goodnature, Sgt. Kip A. Jacoby, Sgt. First Class Marcus V. Muralles, Maj. Stephen C. Reich, Sgt. First Class Michael L. Russell, Chief Warrant Officer Chris J. Scherkenbach, Master Sgt. James W. Ponder III.

"Murph" Part 2

For God so loved the world, that he gave his
one and only Son, That whoever believes in
him shall not perish but have eternal life.

—John 3:16 (NIV)

The Medal of Honor is the United States' highest honor for
valor a serviceman or woman can attain. The Medal of Honor
is not given to a winner. This is an award that is reserved for the
bravest of the brave. Ones who go far and beyond the call of
duty to risk his or her own life. So it is never won. It is awarded
to the recipient by the president of The United States in the
name of Congress for their actions.

The history of the medal can be traced back to Iowa sen-
ator James Grimes. He had the idea to create an award for sea-
men and marines who distinguished themselves by gallantry in
action during the Civil War. Since then, it has gone through
many legislative, design, and presentation changes. It is still,
however, the military's highest award for valor. The first Medal
of Honor was presented to Bernard J. D. Irwin for his actions

February 13, 1861. He was not presented the award until thirty years later. Although there have been over 3,500 Medal of Honor recipients, the award is given out sparingly.

The medal itself is a wonderful work of art. Currently there are three versions on the Medal of Honor, the ribbon of each version is light blue (the color of valor) with thirteen stars embroidered on it representing the thirteen original colonies. The Army's version has an eagle attached to the top of the medal joining the medal to the ribbon. Under it simply is the word valor. Under it is a wreath of laurel leaves. Inside it you find the word United States of America surrounding the central engraving. At its center you find the profile of Minerva, the goddess of wisdom and war. The navy, marine corps, and coast guard version has an anchor attaching the ribbon to the medal. The medal is star shaped with laurel leaves in each of its points. Thirty-four stars can be found encircling the insignia. Each star represents one of the thirty-four states from both the union and confederacy. A different depiction of Minerva can be found at the center of this version. The air force version has the word valor under the ribbon attached to the medal by the coat of arms of the air force. A wreath of laurel leaves encircles this medal as well. Thirty-four stars representing the same thirty-four states can be found encircling the insignia. At the center you find the Statue of Liberty. Each version is a well thought out work of art with symbolism in every detail.

Lt. Murphy was awarded the Medal of Honor posthumously on October 22, 2007. The details of every Medal of Honor recipient are documented in detail. The citation from the Congressional Medal of Honor Society's website reads like this:

> For conspicuous gallantry and intrepid-
> ity at the risk of his life above and beyond
> the call of duty as the leader of a special

reconnaissance element with Naval Special Warfare Task Unit Afghanistan on 27 and 28 June 2005. While leading a mission to locate a high-level anti-coalition militia leader, Lieutenant Murphy demonstrated extraordinary heroism in the face of grave danger in the vicinity of Asadabad, Konar Province, Afghanistan. On 28 June 2005, operating in an extremely rugged enemy-controlled area, Lieutenant Murphy's team was discovered by anti-coalition militia sympathizers who revealed their position to Taliban fighters. As a result, between 30 and 40 enemy fighters besieged his four-member team. Demonstrating exceptional resolve, Lieutenant Murphy valiantly led his men in engaging the large enemy force. The ensuing fierce firefight resulted in numerous enemy casualties, as well as the wounding of all four members of the team. Ignoring his own wounds and demonstrating exceptional composure, Lieutenant Murphy continued to lead and encourage his men. When the primary communicator fell mortally wounded, Lieutenant Murphy repeatedly attempted to call for assistance for his beleaguered teammates. Realizing the impossibility of communicating in the extreme terrain, and in the face of almost certain death, he fought his way into open terrain to gain a better position to transmit a call. This deliberate, heroic act deprived him of cover, exposing him to direct enemy fire. Finally achieving contact with his headquarters, Lieutenant Murphy maintained his exposed position while he provided his location and requested immediate support for his team. In his final act of bravery, he continued to engage the enemy until he was mortally wounded, gallantly giving his life for his country and for the cause of freedom. By his selfless leadership, courageous actions, and extraordinary devotion to duty, Lieutenant Murphy reflected great credit upon himself and upheld the highest traditions of the United States Naval Service.

Lt. Murphy's actions and sacrifice are the reasons he was awarded the Medal of Honor. Becoming another member of this distinguished family.

Sacrifice is the second thing I want to draw your attention to in the story of Lt. Murphy. The act of giving up something that you want to keep especially in order to get or do something else or to help someone is the Merriam-Webster definition of sacrifice. That is exactly what Lt. Murphy did. He sacrificed himself, to try to save his brothers. Not only is it an example of sacrifice, but it is the ultimate example of love. Jesus teaches us this with his words in John 15:13, "Greater love has no one than this, that someone lay down his life for his friends" (ESV). When you truly love someone, you would give everything just to make sure they are okay. No matter the cost, no matter how far you had to go, you would willingly take that journey. Lt. Murphy made that exact choice and demonstrated it in real life. So his brothers could live and stay in the fight he chose to leave cover and safety and his future and make the call for help.

We all like to see ourselves in the story. If we're honest with each other, we like to envision ourselves as the hero. However, in our story and in God's story, we are not the hero. We are the ones who need help. This is not a self-help chapter to encourage you to search within yourself to become the hero. No this is a chapter urging you to accept the fact you need help! Cue up the Bonnie Tyler music 'cause we need a hero to save us. More importantly this chapter is about believing that God in his great love and mercy gave us the hero we don't deserve. Your hero and my hero is Jesus. If we are putting anyone else above him or looking to someone else as our hero, we are setting ourselves up for failure. Before we can ever become an asset for the Lord, we have to accept the fact that we are utterly lost, forever separated from God by the chasm of our own sin, and because of that we are destined to die.

We are not in some tragic story of good people who get put in a bad situation. It is actually the opposite. We are sinful people and because of that sin we are in full rebellion from God. When we do what we want to do over what God wants us to do, in a nutshell, is sin. The Bible tells us in Romans 3:23, "For all have sinned and fall short of the glory of God" (NIV). We cannot place the blame on others. Our parents, spouse, friends, environment, or circumstances cannot be our scapegoat. It's 100 percent on us! Our actions have eternal consequences. The Bible says in Romans 6:23, "For the wages of sin is death, but the free gift of God is eternal life in Christ Jesus our Lord" (ESV). The price of our sin is death. It's one that we all will face. Romans 6:23, though, does not leave us hopeless. Although we deserve death God is freely offering us eternal life in Jesus.

Understanding our need for a savior is great and very important. However, when you put the reason, we need a savior with the understanding of the sacrifice it took to save us, that realization will change your life. Have you ever come to this realization? Or is your faith still knowledge based? Jesus did not come so we could have knowledge of a savior. He came so we could have a relationship with God! Take a moment before we go any further and search your heart. If your faith is knowl-edge-based, ask God right now to show you how to have a personal saving relationship with Jesus. If you do have a relationship with Jesus, I hope and pray that the following paragraphs in this chapter will remind you about God's unfailing love for you. I pray they take you back to the moment when you knew in your heart Jesus died for you so you can live with him. I also hope that it will encourage you to keep running hard after Jesus. If he never gave us anything else other than salvation, then that is still more than enough reason to follow him daily!

First thing we need to look at is that Jesus was fully God and fully man. This is something we cannot just skim over. Being fully God he had the power of God. You see examples of this over and over again in the gospels. He was with God the Father at the beginning of the world, so he is not a character inserted in the middle of the story, He is the main character from the start. This entire narrative is about him and his glory. Being fully God, he did not have to come save us. This was not his right of passage to take the next step toward godhood. He is fully God. Not lacking anything. This is where we find the beauty of the gospel. God, who we rebelled against, sent his son to rescue us. Jesus came from heaven and took on flesh, and with it all the hardships in the world. He left perfection (heaven) where there was no sickness or pain and came and took on all of that and more. For our loved ones, we would travel the world to help them. We would leave the comfort of home to give them a chance; however, for a stranger we won't walk across the street to help. Much less someone who is our enemy. This is exactly what Jesus did for us. While we were still in our sin Jesus came and died for us. Just like Lt Murphy stepping out in the open to make the phone call to save his men, Jesus stepped out of heaven and took on the cross sacrificing himself so we can be saved. It's okay to take a second and praise him for that.

It should have been us who was beaten. It should have been us who was humiliated and shamed. It should have been us who walked the hill of Cavalry. It should have been us who died that day. It was not us, though; it was Jesus. That is the gift that God offers to every person on this Earth. The gift of grace and mercy found in the life and work of Jesus. We can never earn it. Above that we could never pay him back for it. Because of God's love for us he freely offers it to us as a gift. Jesus paid the price for our sin so we can have freedom and redemption in him. His sacrifice allowed us to be made right with God. Paul tells us this in 2 Corinthians 5:21, "God made him who had no sin to be sin for us, so that in him we might become the righteousness of God" (NIV). Take a second and use your imagination with me. Imagine standing in the room with God and Jesus and all the angels. God is about to award Jesus the greatest honor he could give. Instead of putting it on him, God turned and placed it around your neck. You did not earn it. You for sure don't deserve it. Yet here you are with the highest honor. Although only an example this is exactly what happens with us when we accept Jesus as our savior. God takes Jesus is righteousness and places it on us. The best thing we could ever be given is salvation, and God gives it freely to those who believe in him!

How does this work? Is it a twelve labors of Hercules kind of thing? Or a prayer that has to be said exactly right? It's the attitude of our heart. The Bible tells us how to accept God's gift of salvation. "If you declare with your mouth, 'Jesus is Lord,' and believe in your heart that God raised him from the dead, you will be saved" (Rom. 10:9 NIV). It's really that simple. When you claim Jesus as Lord, you are giving him more than a title. You are claiming that he is in charge of your life. You follow him now. It's about his glory and his renown instead of yours. Is Jesus Lord of your life? Are your decisions and actions based on his calling and purpose? Or are you sitting on the throne of your life? Basically, it boils down to this: Is Jesus king of your heart? If he is awesome! If he is not and you want him to be then take a second in prayer and ask him. Be open and honest. Remember God already knows your heart!

The next part is where faith comes in. It's not hard to believe that a man named Jesus of Nazareth was crucified by the Romans. We can find that documented in history. After his death he was placed in a borrowed tomb that was sealed with a large stone. The Jewish leaders were worried someone would steal the body of Jesus and claim he had risen. The Bible tells us on the third day after Jesus died Mary Magdalene and the other Mary had prepared spices for his body and went to the tomb early in the morning. When they got to the tomb, they found the stone rolled away. An angel comes and reminds Mary that Jesus told her this would happen. She then meets Jesus outside the tomb, but does not know it's him. When they realized it was him, they worshiped him. Jesus has that effect on people when they meet him. Then they went and told his disciples. After this Jesus appears to his disciples and many others over forty days before ascending to heaven.

This is the part of the story where our faith is placed as Christians. Even other religions will admit there was a man named Jesus who was a good man and a great teacher. However, they do not admit that he defeated death, or that Hehwas the Son of God. So this is our test of faith, like Indiana Jones in the search for the holy grail has to take a step of faith from solid ground into the chasm, hoping he would not fall to his death. That is exactly what we're doing. Stepping out in faith over the chasm of our sin toward God, and believing that Jesus will catch us. If he had not risen from the grave, this would be asinine. Not only would we be putting our hope in a mad man, but also our faith would be in the biggest liar in history. If he had not risen from the grave, why should we worry about being an asset for the Lord? Without the resurrection, we are still dead in our sins. Paul talks about this in 1 Corinthians 15:29–32:

> Now if there is no resurrection, what will those do who are baptized for the dead? If the dead are not raised at all, why are people baptized for them? And as for us, why do we endanger ourselves every hour? I face death every day—yes, just as surely as I boast about you in Christ Jesus our Lord. If I fought wild beasts in Ephesus with no more than human hopes, what have I gained? If the dead are not raised, "Let us eat and drink, for tomorrow we die." (NIV)

How could we ever expect him to save us if he could not save himself. Our faith is not in a mad man or a liar, but in the one and only son of God. Because of who he is and what he did is the only reason we need to live this life of faith. Sometimes we will ask why we are having to go through trials. Paul even alludes to this in his letter, making the argument that if there is no resurrection of the dead why would you put yourself in danger. That's a good question for us as well. If you don't believe that Jesus has risen from the grave, then trying to live a life to glorify him is silly. More than that, it is pointless.

Jesus is risen from the grave, though. So the biggest question of my life and your life is, what side of the chasm are we going to stand on? Will you continue to stand in your sin and hope to do enough that when you die God lets you into heaven? Or will you step onto the bridge of faith built on the life, death, and resurrection of Jesus Christ of Nazareth?

Remember every special forces operator had to start by joining the military. The same is true for us. So if you have never placed your faith in Jesus, claiming him as Lord of your life, or believing he lived the perfect life, died on the cross to pay the price for your sins, and beat death by rising from the grave, then today is the day. It's the attitude of your heart that matters, but if you are struggling with what to pray try this: "Dear Lord, I am a sinner. Please forgive me! Come into my life and cleanse me of my sin. I believe you sent your son Jesus to die for me, and believe you raised him from the dead. I put my faith, hope, and trust in you alone God. In Jesus's name I pray, amen."

If you said that prayer, congratulations! You just made the best decision of your life! If you are still exploring faith in Jesus, check out these passages from God's Word: Hebrews 11:1, Ephesians 2:8, Galatians 2:20, Galatians 2:16, John 3:16.

"But thanks be to God he gives us the victory through our Lord Jesus Christ" (1 Cor. 15:57).

SITREP

During an operation that the military is conducting the leaders back at the command location need to have an idea about what's going on. This helps to coordinate the rest of the mission. To see if the plan needs to be changed. Or to see if help needs to be sent in. Communication is a key to any successful operation.

Before we go any further, I just wanted to encourage you to sit and evaluate where you are at in this discipleship process. Are you on track? Or have you been living a Christian life of apathy? Just doing the minimum with your relationship with God? I hope that you see through the first half of this book that God wants you to be a tier 1 disciple. He did not call you to be an average follower. Jesus's call was not to come follow me if you have nothing else to do. It was an invitation to become the best version of yourself. Having Jesus as your Lord and Savior is the only way to reach our full God given potential. We know this is true from Jesus's words in John 10:10, "The thief comes only to steal and kill and destroy; I have come that they may have life, and have it to the full" (NIV).

So I just want you to take a second, hour, day, or however long it takes and give a SITREP of your discipleship journey. To help with this I have listed a few questions below for you. Be honest with yourself and with God. Soldiers can't sugar coat

SITREPs while in battle. Just like them we can't risk sugar coating the status of our discipleship journey.

- How has your prayer life been in the last thirty days?
- How much time have you spent in God's Word?
- What has your attitude been like with your family and friends?
- Have your actions been glorifying God?
- Have you let fear take you out of the fight?
- Are you living for your glory or God's?

The most important question of the SITREP is simply this. In the last few chapters I hope you have seen that God loved you so much that he gave his son Jesus for you. I hope you know that Jesus is our only way to a relationship with God. So *have you put your faith and trust in Jesus to be your Lord and savior?*

If your answer for that is anything other than *yes*, then all of the other lessons in this book will not matter. It's not about living a good life, it is about living a life with God! Understand that no matter how good of a life you live, if that life is apart from Jesus, then you missed it. I heard an example one time from a preacher where he said he read an article on a billionaire. He was asked what he would tell his younger self if he could go back and give himself some advice. The billionaire said he would tell his younger self that it is empty at the top. Please don't miss it. Please don't put all your eggs in the world's basket, hoping it will satisfy you. Remember Jesus is our way, truth, and life.

Take however long you need. Know that you have been prayed for as you take this time to evaluate your walk with Jesus. When you're ready, let's continue the mission of becoming the disciple God made you to be!

6

The Only Easy Day Was Yesterday

Not only so, but we also glory in our sufferings,
because we know that suffering produces perseverance;
perseverance, character; and character, hope.

—Romans 5:3–4

Every person of the special forces community had to earn the right to become a member. Earning that title is no walk in the park. Whether it's SEALS, Green Berets, Marine Raiders, or the SAS, the pipeline is a hard journey to say the least. Which path is the hardest depends on who you ask. Below I have listed a few of the pipelines toward special forces for some of the branches of the military. I'll let you decide for yourself who you think is the toughest.

Let's start out with the air force special warfare division. There are four different careers that all hold the title of special warfare; combat controllers (CCT), pararescue (PJs), Special Reconnaissance (SR), tactical air control party (TACP). The basics of the pipeline look like this. The entire length of the air force special warfare pipeline is about seventy-nine weeks. That is split up into different sections such as recognizance training, SEAR (survival, evasion, resistance, and escape) training as well as many others. The Army's Green berets pipeline can be anywhere from fifty-three to ninety-five weeks long. This depends on the MOS of the soldier. They have the same option of choosing between different careers in the special forces family.

Just like the air force the army special forces candidates go through a prep and selection course. After that they must complete the Q course. It has six different sections and concludes with the Robin Sage exercise in the North Carolina mountains. This tests their training to succeed in the world of unconventional warfare.

Marine Corps Special Forces (MARSOC) begins selection and assessment courses followed by a nine-month special operations individual course (ITC). The ITC is broken up into four phases ranging from small unit tactics to irregular warfare.

The last special operations training we will look at more in depth is the Navy's SEALS. The pipeline begins with Naval Special Warfare prep school. This is a two-month focus on basic skill and physical fitness. Then the cadets get assigned to a class and begin BUDS (Basic Underwater Demolition/SEAL training) The first step of BUDS is phase 1 that focuses on physical training and water competence. It is in this phase where each person will go through the famous "Hell Week." In phase 2 it is all about the water. Where SEAL candidates become basic combat swimmers. They also learn open- and closed-circuit diving. In phase 3, SEAL candidates focus on land warfare. Training doesn't end with phase 3. All the candidates who pass each phase are then sent to SEAL Qualification Training. There they learn how to work in a SEAL platoon. After all this is when the candidates earn their trident.

The goal of each phase is to see which cadet will measure up both mentally and physically to the SEAL standard. There is a high attrition rate in each class. Although the class starts with big numbers, they always finish with very few members. That is exactly what the Navy wants; to find the ones who are physically, and more importantly mentally tough enough to earn the trident. It is during these phases where one of the mottos of Navy Seals is sewn into the DNA of every man. The only easy day was yesterday.

Take phase 1 for example. Every day is hard and challenging. Each week you do more running, swimming, and exercises than the week before. Soldiers are tested on a four-mile run in the soft sand, two-mile swims in the cold Pacific Ocean, plus completion of the obstacle course. Majority of the time, while completing each evolution, the men are cold, wet, and sandy. Now I don't know about you, but I don't want to run four miles with sand on every crevice of my body. Then each man must complete "Hell Week." This evolution is a five-and-a-half-day stretch where the cadets sleep a total of about four hours during that time span. Cadets also run about two hundred miles that week paired with physical training twenty hours a day.

The training of the SEALS is well documented. So each man knows what's coming. At any point during the training the men have the option to DOR (drop on request). So at any point that a soldier reaches their limit, they can stop the physical and mental test/abuse. All they have to do is ring the bell. The option to quit is always there. Most of the time they are being reminded that all they have to do to make the punishment stop is quit.

So how do these guys make it through BUDS? The answer can be found in the motto "The only easy day was yesterday." This simple mindset is the key to making it through. I have heard many different interviews with SEALS where they are all asked the same question: "How did you make it through?." The answer is always close to the same. The guys who just focus on making it to the next task are the ones who make it. The guys who are focused on the end and getting the trident rarely make it. This separation does not have anything to do with physical stature or athleticism. It has everything to do with mindset and mental toughness. By focusing on the task right in front of them they are able keep moving on. They remember that the only easy day they will have was the previous one. The reason it's easy is because they have already completed it. This is a truth and a mindset that everyone of us can gain from implementing in our life.

Have you ever had a bad day? Or a bad week? Or maybe even a bad year? If we're honest, everyone has. It's so easy to get in the mindset of defeat and what I like to call the "whatevers." Let me explain. When bad things happen to us, it's easy to focus on the negative. When we do that, we become more and more defeated mentally. We also can slide into the mindset of "the whatevers." This is where you when you see the task at hand or what your current circumstances look like, your self-talk starts to sound something like this: "I know I need to do this but I will probably just mess it up, or something will go wrong—ugh, whatever." This is a dangerous place to be. The poor me/whatevers kind of mindset and self-talk is the on ramp toward depression and defeat. On *Mental Health America's* website, they report that in 2019 19.88 percent of adults experienced mental illness, while also finding that 4.58 percent of adults report have suicidal thoughts. That's some serious numbers, but each number represents a mom or dad, brother or sister, friend or coworker who is struggling. Maybe that's you. It's okay if you are in that space today, but you do not have to live there. Remember you're not alone in this struggle. I tell my wife all the time it's okay to visit the blues, everyone does. We just can't build a house and live there. Let's look at how we can take the "only easy day was yesterday" mindset and team it with truth from God's Word to help us get through the bad days, weeks, months, or even years.

Having the "only easy day was yesterday" mindset is important to every follower of Jesus. Because Jesus himself said that the path of following him is hard! We see this in Matthew's Gospel. Matthew 8:18–20 tells us:

> Now when Jesus saw a crowd around him, he gave orders to go over to the other side. And a scribe came up and said to him, "Teacher, I will follow you wherever you go." And Jesus said to him, "Foxes have holes, and birds of the air have nests, but the Son of Man has nowhere to lay his head." (ESV)

You must understand that in America, we live in a blessed country. We are able to openly proclaim the name of Jesus. This has not been true for past Christians and current Christians in other parts of the world. In the time of the Roman empire Christians were tried and prosecuted and often put to death. In the days of the early Church, they were used as human torches for the Romans. Even today in some countries Christians have to meet in secret because of the fear of being arrested for worshiping Jesus. So Jesus did not promise us rosy circumstances. We must understand that this journey of following him is tough. Jesus did not tell us to pick up our La-Z-boy and follow him; no, he said pick up your cross. He did, however, promise the destination was worth the journey. So as Christians, we have a reason to go on this journey.

The mindset goes deeper than just openly proclaiming Jesus. We must understand hard times are coming. If we want to be an asset for the Lord, we must be mentally prepared for it. As Christians we should expect hard times. We even must go a step further and embarrass them because they strengthen our faith. Romans 5:3–5 tells us,

> Not only that, but we rejoice in our sufferings, knowing that suffering produces endurance, and endurance produces character, and character produces hope, and hope does not put us to shame, because God's love has been poured into our hearts through the Holy Spirit who has been given to us. (ESV)

Just like how the rigor and trials of BUDS and other special operations training produces mental and physical endurance to handle the next evolution, the trials of life produce the endurance of our faith to handle the situations that arise in life.

We can't skip over what Paul tells us in Romans 5:5, that endurance and character produce hope. Let me try to help you wrap your head around this. If you are going through a hard time or have been, you may be thinking that hallmark wisdom sounds good but is not practical. Catchy sayings sound great but they never make the problem go away. This is not a guide about getting rid of your problems. This is a blueprint of how to handle bad circumstances. We need this because it's easy to quit. Just like in BUDS, when life gets hard, all you have to do to quit is ring the bell. Ring the bell and you can walk away. In life, however, you are not just walking away from an opportunity when you quit, you are walking away from a family, or friends, or coworkers. God does not want you to ring the bell! He wants the exact opposite. He wants your faith to be battle hardened, and tough as nails.

Now that we understand the need for this mindset, we can look at the implementation of it. The foundation has to be this: God is our refuge and strength in the hard times. God will never leave us or forsake us. God does not call you to sit in your weakness, He calls you to stand in his strength. He is big enough to cast your problems on. Above anything else God cares about what you're going through. Our struggles are not hidden from the Lord. We also have hope that all of these things are true, because God is a man of his word. This hope is the fuel that propels us through the hard time to the ultimate goal, heaven. The Bible clearly proclaims these truths about God. Let's look at a few examples. Philippians 4:13 lets us know who gives us strength in all situations: "I can do all this through him who gives me strength" (NIV). Psalm 9:9–10 shows us who is our refuge in rough times: "The Lord is a refuge for the oppressed, a stronghold in times of trouble. Those who know your name trust in you, for you, Lord, have never forsaken those who seek you." First Peter 5:7 tells us God cares about our issues: "Cast all your anxiety on him because he cares for you" (NIV). The scriptures tell us these truths over and over again. If you want to get to know God more, open up your Bible. As you learn more about who God is and his character, your relationship with him strengthens.

Hope is how we apply this mindset to our life. We know that the only easy day was yesterday, and that hard challenges are coming down the line of our life. We can face every challenge head on because of Jesus and our hope in him. Hope that is based on Jesus will never be found lacking. Jesus walked on water, healed the blind, raised the dead, and beat death Himself. So no matter how bad the circumstance is that is staring you in the face, Jesus is more than capable to handle it. The question is do you trust him enough to let Him? Will you let that hope impact your attitude and character?

This mindset can help on a small-scale issue or a large scale. A lot of times it's the small-scale battles that we lose. We allow the negative to impact our attitude. It does not have to be that way, though. I found this out on a random Monday night in the winter of 2021. I had been working at the softball field trying to get the indoor facility ready for the season. When I got home, it was around six o'clock. After playing with the kids and getting them ready for bed, my wife says, "Hey, the sink is not draining, and it kinda is starting to stink. I bought a drain cleaner the other day. Can we try to use it?" Now I know as much plumbing as I do Latin, so this was not in my comfort zone. However, I thought, *How hard can this be?* I have two degrees, dang it; I can figure this out! Well, after trying the drain cleaner and nothing happening, I decided to take the pipe off to see if it was clogged (we're now at eight-thirty-ish). After cleaning up the water up off the floor that spilled when I took the pipe off, I found the problem. That problem was wet and smelled like it died a few times. Getting it out should have required a hazmat suit. I did not have one. Nor did I have any gloves, but the job had to be completed. There was no sound track playing that night, but if there was it would have sounded something like this… There goes my hero, watch him as he goes. At least in my mind that's what was playing. After getting the pipes put back together (praise the Lord) and washing my hands for a while, the job was done. The mission was accomplished! For me that is a perfect situation for frustration. I was not really sure how to do what I was trying to do, and the closest outlet for that frustration was my family. Fixing the sink that night was the last thing I wanted to do. Before I started, I took a deep breath and thought about the Navy SEAL motto. I tried to attack it as an opportunity not an obstacle. This is how we honor God in tough situations, with our attitudes toward him and the people around us. The only easy day mindset can remind us to honor God in tough situations.

Now I know that unclogging a sink is not a big life issue, but the mindset translates to the major life moments. Knowing that the only easy day was yesterday can help you honor God and love others. It can empower us to show grace on hard days because Jesus showed grace on hard days. We attack the situation as an opportunity to honor God, even when life deals us a bad hand. I want you to understand that life will not be fun at times. At the end of the day, though, whatever the situation is, it has to be handled. More so just like in special operations training, the situation has to be completed and done to the standard.

Now I don't know what you are walking through right now. One of my best friends from college used to say, in life, you are either going into a storm or coming out of one. I do want to encourage you to attack the big and small problems with this mindset. Remember that God cares about our conduct in the circumstances. Jesus told us that loving God and loving others is the most important thing we can do. That's not just on the easy days. That's an all-day, everyday objective for Christians to accomplish. If you are having a problem with the "poor mes" or the whatevers, spend some time in prayer asking God to help you. Just because it's the way you have been does not mean it is the way you have to be. I pray that God will help you and me carry this mindset into all areas of our lives.

Try to store Matthew 14:22–33 in your heart and remember Jesus will call you to him in the storm, and if you start to sink, he will save you!

Obstacle or opportunity, the choice is yours.

Keep It Simple

And he said to him, "You shall love the Lord your God with
all your heart and with all your soul and with all your mind.
This is the great and first commandment. And a second is
like it: You shall love your neighbor as yourself. On these
two commandments depend all the Law and the Prophets.

—Matthew 22:37–40

On the afternoon of December 7, 1941, president Franklin D.
Roosevelt addressed the nation after the attack on Pearl Harbor.
His words that day have echoed through the decades. They
also have defined one of the darkest days in American History.
Any good history student can connect the phrase President
Roosevelt used in his address to describe the events that fateful
day to the attack on Pearl Harbor. That horrible day in history springboarded a nation into a global conflict, while alter-
ing the course of many Americans' lives. I remember talking
to my grandfather about it, and how it impacted his life. Once
America entered the war, they started up the draft. He knew
he would get drafted so instead of waiting he enlisted in the

Merchant Marines on his own. They sent him to Kings Point, New York, to the Merchant Marine Academy. That was never his plan until after December 7, 1941. That is just a personal example of what thousands of Americans faced because of the attack on Pearl Harbor by the Japanese.

For my generation, the day that will live in infamy was September 11, 2001. That day terrorist's hijacked multiple passenger jets and used them to attack the World Trade Centers and the Pentagon. I remember watching it in my eighth-grade classroom, thinking this looks like a bad movie. The actions that day, just like the attack on Pearl Harbor, altered the history of America. President Bush went to ground zero a few days after the attacks and addressed all of the first responders working to try to find survivors. As he is talking (using a bullhorn), someone yells, "We can't hear you." President Bush turns and responds and says, "I can hear you, the rest of the world hears you, and the people who knocked these buildings down will hear all of us soon." Just like President Roosevelt's address on December 7, 1941, President Bush's words have echoed through the decades as well.

President Bush's words that day were not an empty promise. America responded with Operation Enduring Freedom and that became the Global War on Terror. Just to put in perspective let's look at some of the facts and figures from the Afghanistan War. Ellen Kinckmeyer of the Associated Press listed these figures from her article on August 16, 2021. Over 2,400 US service members lost their lives in Afghanistan. Over 47,00 Afghanistan civilians lost their lives along with over 51,000 Taliban and other opposition fighters. Also 444 aid workers along with seventy-two journalists also lost their lives during this conflict. The estimated cost of the war is two trillion dollars. That's a two with twelve zeros behind it (2,000,000,000,000). That does not count the war in Iraq that started a few years after this operation began.

It also started the greatest manhunt in the history of the world. Al Qaeda and its leader Osama bin Laden took the credit for the attack of 9/11. The American intelligence agencies began trying to track down all of the leaders of Al Qaeda with special focus on capturing or killing Osama bin Laden. This man hunt took nearly a decade. However, through the work of the intelligence agencies, bin Laden was finally found and killed by a team of Navy SEALS in May of 2011. The raid on bin Laden's compound in Abbottabad, Pakistan, will be our focus for this chapter.

There were many different options for President Obama to choose from, once the intelligence community believed that the high value target (HVT) in the compound was bin Laden. A special operations raid was on the table. As well as different bombing options. However, the risk of collateral damage eventually led to the decision to use the special operations raid. This operation was named "Operation Neptune's Spear."

Now Operation Neptune's Spear has been well documented in print, as well as different movies. I would like to draw our connections for this chapter from the account of the Commanding Officer Admiral William McRaven. Admiral McRaven details this operation in his book *Sea Stories: My Life In Special Operations*. This is a great read for anyone who loves the history of Special Warfare. For our journey, we can learn a lot from the planning of this mission as well as the speech McRaven gave the operators right before the raid. From the different ideas of how to capture or kill bin Laden, to McRaven's use of his thesis on rehearsing everything. We can draw connections from these lessons and apply them to our Christian lives. The first lesson I want us to look at is from the speech Admiral McRaven gave to the operators before they conducted the raid on the Abbottabad compound.

Understand this was no simple raid. Pakistan was kept out of the loop about the operation. Bin Laden's compound was also right down the road from Pakistan's military academy and Abbottabad's police station. On top of that the intelligence agencies could not say with 100 percent certainty that it was bin Laden in the compound. The target was just known as "the pacer." So here goes this team of SEALS across the Pakistan border on a capture/kill mission of an unverified HVT, mixed in with the thought that it could be the man responsible for thousands of American lives. It's only natural that the operators could feel the weight of this mission. Not only was this the most wanted man in the world, but also the risk of ending up in a Pakistani prison was real if the operators were captured. No pressure, right?

The tactics of the mission were simple. Entrance, breaching, clearing rooms and apprehending/subduing subjects, collecting intelligence, were something these operators had done hundreds of times in Afghanistan and other parts of the Middle East during the global war on terror. That is the message that Admiral McRaven wanted to get across to the team of SEALs. So he uses an example from a famous scene in the movie *Hoosiers*. *Hoosiers* is a movie about the journey of a small-town basketball team, and their coach, to the state championship. When the team walks into the gym, they would play for the championship in, the coach (Gene Hackman) breaks out the tape measure. He gets the kids to measure the height of the goal, and the length of the court. He tells them if they did the same thing back in Hickory the measurements would be the same. The point of the message was to play their game. Don't change what you do when the stage gets bigger. McRaven told the SEALs, "Don't change your tactics, and play your game."

Now we know from accounts of how the raid goes. Although not everything went according to the original plan, the mission was a success. Osama bin Laden was killed in Operation Neptune's Spear. The biggest manhunt in the history of the world had finally ended. I remember when the news broke in America. I was on a bus coming back from a softball game when Coach McGinnis cut the news on the TV. Everyone started clapping and cheering. You would have thought we had knocked off the number one team in the country with the way we were acting. I can still see the television coverage of the people outside the White House chanting, "USA, USA, USA." As great of a moment as this was, it could never bring back the 2,977 lives that were lost on that September day. For me personally, and I could bet for many Americans it felt like a small piece of closure. Even though the War on Terror was still raging on in the Middle East with thousands of American sons and daughters down range, this was a big victory for the people of the United States.

As Christians, it would be wise of us to take the advice that Admiral McRaven gave the operators before the raid. Keep it simple and play your game! So often in our world today people (me and you) have become experts in making a mountain out of a molehill. If you don't believe me, just scroll through your Facebook newsfeed. Listen to your coworkers at the water cooler. When the big moments do come up in life, we let the stress and worry often overrun our mind. We also overcomplicate the purpose and mission of our life. We spend too much energy and focus on things that will not matter in one hundred years. Not to mention the over complication of our relationships. Reading too much into every little thing. Comparing our relationships to the ones we see on social media. Living this way is as far from keeping it simple as you can get.

What does that advice have to do with the gospel? As Christians, what is "our game"? How do we keep it simple when a loved one is diagnosed with cancer? Or how do we respond when we lose a job? How do we act when we get overlooked or passed over for a promotion? Well, luckily for us Jesus lays out the only plan of action Christians need. It's so simple and always allows us to keep things and situations in perspective. In the twenty-second chapter of the Gospel of Matthew we find Jesus being questioned by the Jewish teachers and leaders. First, they asked him about paying taxes. Then they asked him about marriage and the resurrection. Finally, they asked him what is the greatest commandment? The enemy can use the same tactic against us today. By trying to get you to focus on the red tape of religion. It is our job to remain focused on the love and grace found in a relationship with God. Jesus shows us how to do this with his response in Matthew 22:34–40:

> Hearing that Jesus had silenced the Sadducees, the Pharisees got together. One of them, an expert in the law, tested him with this question: "Teacher, which is the greatest commandment in the Law?" Jesus replied: "'Love the Lord your God with all your heart and with all your soul and with all your mind.' This is the first and greatest commandment. And the second is like it: 'Love your neighbor as yourself.' All the Law and the Prophets hang on these two commandments. (NIV)

Now you may be thinking that love God and love others is too simple to fix the problems in my life. I understand what you are thinking. That simple solutions to complex problems sound like an oxymoron. Try to look at it like this. Imagine you have a beautiful watch. You wear it every day to every occasion. One day the watch starts having issues. You open the back and see all the parts and gears and realize you have no clue where to even begin. What any normal person would do is look at the instructions. The best place to find out how to fix the watch is from the maker of the watch. The same is true for our lives. The best place to find the resolution to the problems we face, is the maker of heaven and Earth. We find out at the beginning of Genesis that God created the heavens and Earth. The Bible also tells that God knit us together in our mother's womb. "For you formed my inward parts; you knitted me together in my mother's womb" (Ps. 139:13 ESV). God is familiar with the smallest detail of our life down to the atomic level. It is in our best interest to trust his instructions. God's simple approach is to love him and love others.

Most of the time, the tough situations in life arise without warning. Now if we could go into our war room and plan out how to react to every person and situation, the world would be a better place. The problem is most of our issues are TSTs (time-sensitive targets). So the best plan of action should be simple and easy to execute. That is exactly what the advice Jesus gave us is, simple and easy to execute on a daily basis.

One of my favorite sayings I have picked up from the journey of this book is "work the problem." When an issue or a situation in life comes up, the best path to a solution or resolution is to work the problem. Talking about the problem can make us feel better, but the problem is still there. If we ignore the problem, it never goes away and usually gets worse. The issue facing most people is they don't know how to begin to work the problem. The best plan of action is always the simplest to execute. It should be a tactic you have practiced and used time and time again. You may be thinking dropping a bomb on my situation/problem is the simplest solution. That was the same thing that President Obama was presented with as an option on how to get Osama bin Laden. However, any-time you blow something up, there will always be the chance of collateral damage. Minimizing that should always be a top priority in our life.

When Admiral McRaven spoke to the pilots before the raid, he gave them simple instructions. If something goes wrong before the operation begins, just get the operators on the ground. They are trained to work the problem so just get them on the ground so they can do their job. The same is true for us. When an issue arises, we feel like we must correct it right then. Although it sounds good at the moment, sometimes we just need to get it on the ground. Once we do that, we can then use the teaching and lessons of Jesus to work whatever problem is in front of us to get back on mission as quickly and easily as possible. Sometimes working the problem can be quick, and sometimes it can take longer than we think. That process can't start until we get the bird on the ground. This is exactly what the pilots did in the UBL raid, and because of their action and skill the operators were able to work the problem when the plan had to be changed. Because of their actions and the skills of the operators, the mission was completed.

The first step Jesus shows us is the most important. That is to love God with all your heart, mind, strength, and all your soul. This should always be the foundation of everything we do as Christians. Just like the SEALs relied on the training and fundamentals that they executed thousands of times to successfully complete Operation Neptune's Spear, we should rely on our fundamental of loving God with all we have all the time. Our heart and soul have to be all in all the time for this to be effective in our life. When that changes in our life is when we get in trouble. The entire Old Testament tells that exact story; God loves people and blesses them, people turn from God and turn to idols and rebellion (stop loving him with all they have), problems and hard times come, people turn back to God and leave their idols, God forgives and loves the people. When you love God with everything you have, there is no room in your heart for idols. Jesus teaches us that our love for God should make our love for anything else look like hate. What that means is if the world compares your love of God to your love of anything else, the love for anything else will look like hate. I know this sounds crazy but one of my favorite pastors David Platt explains it like this. It's not that you hate your mom and dad or spouse or friends. It's if we compared how much we love Jesus to them that it would look like we hate them, because our love for Jesus is so overwhelming.

When we are all in all the time on loving God with all we have, our life begins to change. Our relationship with our spouse and family begins to look different. Our work ethic changes for the better. We also will become better friends. Let me explain how this happens. As we love God with all we have, we are able to love our spouses and families more deeply, by understanding it is our duty to love them as Jesus loves us. Because of our relationship with God, our understanding of what true love is begins to grow and mature. The quality of our work and our work ethic improve as well, because we strive to bring God glory in everything we do, working for his glory not ours. The more you love God the more you want to make him proud. Our friendships evolve because when you love God with everything you realize what true friendship is. You want to be a better friend because you see how much of a friend Jesus is to us. One objective we can all strive to complete every day is simply this: Let every aspect of our lives look as much like Jesus as we can.

The second step Jesus gives us builds off the first. As we love God with all we have, we cannot help but love others. This goes further than our family and friends. We are to love our neighbor as ourselves. What does this look like in a practical sense? How should we interact with the world around us? How should we treat the people outside our circle of friends and family? The answer to these can be found in another question; what would Jesus do? This question is more than just a bracelet some people wear. We should interact with the world around us showing love and compassion and grace to the undeserving because that's what Jesus did. Paul speaks about what Jesus would do in Romans 5:7–8: "Very rarely will anyone die for a righteous person, though for a good person someone might possibly dare to die. But God demonstrates his own love for us in this: While we were still sinners, Christ died for us" (NIV). If God would die for us while we were sinners, then we must love others as he loves us. We find out what this l can look like in our life as we love God with everything we have, and spend time with him. The more you read and study about the life of Jesus, then the better understanding you will have of how to live like Jesus.

Jesus, again, does not leave us guessing. In his sermon on the mount (Matt. 5–7) Jesus shows us what that looks like with the beatitudes. If we're honest, we usually read this as a transaction between us and God. Meaning if we do (x) then God will bless us with (y). Just like if you give a store (x) amount of money, then they will give you the product or service (y) that you want. Kenneth Bailey describes in his book *Jesus Through Middle Eastern Eyes* that it's actually the opposite. It's not that you will be blessed, it is you already are blessed if you do these things. We are not doing these things to increase our spiritual bank accounts. The Bible tells us that we have already been given every blessing under heaven. "Praise be to the God and Father of our Lord Jesus Christ, who has blessed us in the heavenly realms with every spiritual blessing in Christ" (Eph. 1:3). So God has already filled our spiritual bank accounts when we accept Jesus as our Lord and Savior. So we live this way because of those blessings not for more blessings.

The second lesson we can learn for Operation Neptune's Spear is you can't plan for everything. The government made a full-scale model of the compound for the operators and pilots to rehearse. The problem with this was that the compound was to scale but the walls were different. So when the HALO hovered above the compound, it lost control and crashed. However, because of the skill of the pilot all members on board were okay and able to continue. Even though the plan of attack had to change, the operators relied on their fundamental tactics. As Christians, we must attack our problems the same way. When life throws a wrench in our plan, we must always fall back on the fundamental tactics Jesus taught us. We can't rehearse and prepare for everything, so our fundamentals have to be our focus.

The question for us today is will we implement Jesus's instructions all the time or only when it's convenient. In simpler terms, will you keep it simple? The world is trying to tell you that part of the time is pretty good. Remember God is not calling you to be pretty good. Keeping it simple and playing our game is something we can all improve on. So I want to encourage you to work on the fundamentals daily. When the big missions of life come up, loving God and loving others will be something you have executed thousands of times. My hope and prayer for my life and yours is that when God calls us every morning to love him and love others with all we have, our response will be "Roger that, sir."

On our journey from complexity to simpleness, stick to Jesus's instructions. The most important thing you can do is love God with all you have, and love others. So I want to encourage you to spend time with Jesus daily. Learn more about him, and strive to be more like him. So when the big missions of life come up, you are ready! Our hope is not built on our actions, but rather in the love, mercy, and grace of the Lord, so trust in his commands.

"Be strong and take heart, all of you who hope in the Lord" (Ps. 31:24 NIV).

8

Who Dares Wins

Be on your guard; stand firm in the
faith; be courageous; be strong.

—1 Corinthians 16:13 (NIV)

Growing up in Alabama was awesome! We live near the river and the woods. Not only could we play on the water, but we could also explore the woods. A twelve-year-old on a four-wheeler in the woods, or on a Sea-Doo on the open river is one of the best examples of freedom you can find. For me and my best friend Cameron, it was always an adventure. Either on the water or the woods we were always up to something. Most of the time it was stuff that would get us in trouble. We were always looking to jump off something into the water. One time, we decided to ride our bikes into the river. We thought we were being smart by tying a rope to the bike and the pier. We never accounted for the slack, but we did not lose the bikes. Our ideas always involved a conversation that sounded like this:

"Dude, you go first."

"No, brother, you go first!"
"Dude, I dare you to go first!"
"Why should I go first?"
"Because if something happens to you, I will call 911."

Whoever went first, the other was always right behind them. There was always a dare and an opportunity.

The motto "Who dares wins" belongs to the British Special Air Service (SAS). The SAS are Great Britain's special warfare division. Sometimes a motto or a nickname can just sound cool and not embody the ones who dawn it. Like Ted Mosby on *How I Met Your Mother* calling himself Teddy Westside, or Doink the clown claiming he is the greatest wrestler of all time. Each example sounds good, but they are far from the truth. With the SAS motto they hit the nail right on the head. Daring, courage, and boldness are the attributes that built the SAS.

David Sterling had the idea for a smaller fighting force to attack the Germans in North Africa during World War II. An unconventional unit full of unconventional men. Sterling was a living example of that description. As an officer in the British Royal Army, he was classified as ordinary, but his ideas were revolutionary. Part of his plan was being able to parachute behind enemy lines. The problem with this is Sterling was not a trained airborne soldier. So to fix this problem, he gets a parachute and a plane and takes a jump. He survived this endeavor but his reward for his bravery was broken legs. During his recovery he goes to command to pitch his idea (reportedly using his crutches to break in) and some of the upper brass believe he could be onto something with his radical idea. Romel and the Germans were having their way in North Africa. So new ideas for how to gain the upper hand were needed. Not everyone was all in on Sterling's unconventional warfare, though. Remember innovation will always be met with some type of resistance.

Sterling went to create a detachment in North Africa where the Germans were in control. Sterling's plan was to parachute behind Rommel and the Germans and attack their planes and airfields and sneak back into the desert before anyone knew what happened. Now before this could happen, they needed to train how to jump out of a plane. The problem was the British Army did not give them a plane to train with. To solve the problem, they would jump out of the back of trucks going thirty to forty miles per hour. To be daring you have to be brave, and those men were just that.

Sometimes being daring means to jump into uncomfortable situations. This describes the first mission of the SAS. On the day of the mission, the weather in North Africa was bad. A storm had come up, and created an environment that was not even close to ideal for jumping out of a plane. That is exactly what the SAS did, though. With that kind of bravery and boldness the SAS had success in North Africa. They were always daring to evolve and change. The SAS took part in many operations in World War II, most of the time behind enemy lines. The history and impact of the SAS can be seen from North Africa in 1941 to present day operations all around the world, living up to the motto "Who dares wins." The SAS also had later influence on American special operation groups.

We need to understand that if we are going to take this journey of tier 1 Christianity we must be daring, bold, and brave. I want us to look at two different examples of people who embodied each of these characteristics in the Bible, and the impact it had on them. The first for personal reasons, and the second for a friend. Each is a great example of how God calls us to live a life that is daring, and victorious.

The first example is found in the gospel of Luke when we meet the woman who had a disease for twelve years.

> And a woman was there who had been subject to bleeding for twelve years, but no one could heal her. She came up behind him and touched the edge of his cloak, and immediately her bleeding stopped. "Who touched me?" Jesus asked. When they all denied it, Peter said, "Master, the people are crowding and pressing against you." But Jesus said, "Someone touched me; I know that power has gone out from me." Then the woman, seeing that she could not go unnoticed, came trembling and fell at his feet. In the presence of all the people, she told why she had touched him and how she had been instantly healed. Then he said to her, "Daughter, your faith has healed you. Go in peace. (Luke 8:43–48 NIV)

Now with all the brave examples to look at in the Bible, why look at this woman? As bold and brave as Moses, David, Daniel, and others were, this woman shows us how to live daringly for the Lord. It is exactly what every follower of Jesus should strive to do.

We need to try to understand what this woman went through, not only physically, but mentally and spiritually as well. Physically this constant bleeding had to take a toll on her body. Some translations describe it as hemorrhaging. It was more than just the physical pain and discomfort, though. Always having to physically change clothes would get old after twelve years. Mentally the woman had to be exhausted. Going from place to place looking for healing and always coming up empty would deflate you mentally. She was dealing with disappointment as well as isolation. She would have been an outcast in Jesus's time, where her community would look at her as being unclean or dirty. It's not a stretch to think she would have struggled with a sense of belonging. Spiritually, I can imagine it was worse for her. Hard to go to church, hard to worship, even harder to talk to God, especially with asking God what she did wrong to deserve her problem. It is easy to see just how daring and brave she was in this moment. Pushing through a crowd of the very people who look down on her to get to the spiritual teacher Jesus. She brought nothing in that crowd but shame and guilt, but mixed with that she also brought hope: hope that Jesus was different from the others. And that he could heal her.

We see in the exchange between her and Jesus that not only did her faith heal her physically, but she also found belonging when Jesus calls her "daughter." So at the feet of Jesus, she found instant peace and belonging. The same is true for us. Jesus is inviting us into the family of God. A family where your dad is the creator and ruler of the world. How awesome is that!

Each of us would benefit from being as daring as this woman. No matter what physical problems we have we should boldly bring them to the feet of Jesus. We should also dare to bring our self-image to Jesus. Some people's biggest enemy is the person looking at them in the mirror, and struggling to understand how anyone could love you. Body image is not just a problem for women. Men can struggle with physical insecurity too. We must remember while looking in the mirror that we are fearfully and wonderfully made in the image of the God of the universe. What God says about us, and thinks about us should be the only opinion that we listen to. This is not an excuse to not take care of yourself physically. It's really more of encouragement to do just that. Because we are made in the image of God, we should strive to treat our body like a holy temple. Remember the Holy Spirit lives in you!

Mentally, we should bring our issues to the feet of Jesus. This is a problem for a lot of people. It is hard to admit you are struggling mentally. It takes guts to go to the doctor and say something is not right. Yet the number of Americans who take medication for mental issues is growing by the year. I am not advocating not to take medicine. Medicine can help you be better for your family, friends, and the world around you. I am saying, though, we can't look for our peace from a pill. Because the pill wears off, and then you need another one and another one (I hope as you read that you use your DJ Khaled voice, if not then hopefully you did just now). Yes, it helps, but if you stop taking them you are right back to rock bottom. With God, we can find full peace, where we depend on God to fully satisfy us. Look at it like this: imagine you are going on a trip across the Atlantic Ocean. What takes you across the sea is the boat and its captain. That is who you put your faith in (God and Jesus). If you get seasick, though, you take a pill to help. You can't enjoy the voyage if you are stuck in your room, sick. You don't want to look up and realize you missed it. The joy is in the journey. So it may take medicine for some people to be able to enjoy the journey of this life, and that's okay. Just make sure your faith is still in the captain. Notice how the woman said in front of everyone what Jesus had done. Not worried about what others were thinking, but able to proclaim what God had done in her life. That is a good mental space to live in. Where we can be open about our issues because we understand they are a platform to proclaim the goodness of God.

Will we be daring in our spiritual life? Maybe you are struggling like the woman in the story. Struggling with going to church, worshiping individually and in groups, and talking to God. When we have issues that impact each of these areas, will we be daring enough to come to Jesus? It's easy to stay in the shadows. God, however, is calling us out of the darkness through the crowds to Jesus. If we want to be an elite asset of God, we must be daring like this woman.

The second example we will look at shows how daring we must be for the people around us. This example is also found in the gospel of Luke.

> On one of the days while Jesus was teaching, some proud religious law-keepers and teachers of the Law were sitting by Him. They had come from every town in the countries of Galilee and Judea and from Jerusalem. The power of the Lord was there to heal them. Some men took a man who was not able to move his body to Jesus. He was carried on a bed. They looked for a way to take the man into the house where Jesus was. But they could not find a way to take him in because of so many people. They made a hole in the roof over where Jesus stood. Then they let the bed with the sick man on it down before Jesus. When Jesus saw their faith, He said to the man, "Friend, your sins are forgiven. (Luke 5:17–20 NIV)

This is one of the best examples of the impact a daring life for Jesus can have on the people around you.

Let's look at the text to understand just how daring these guys were. Jesus had a following because of the miracles he was performing. People would come from all over to hear him teach and watch him heal people. Even the religious elite would come to see Jesus. Luke's Gospel tells us that he was in a house and it was full of people. These guys cared so much about the man and what he was going through that they actually carried him to Jesus. That is the kind of daring attitude followers of Jesus need. Most of the time, our friends and family will not be willing to go to church to hear about Jesus on their own. Will we be daring enough to carry them? To go out of our way to bring them to Jesus. Then will we be daring enough to not take no for an answer? These guys could not get into the house where Jesus was. So they made a way by cutting a hole in the roof and lowering him to Jesus. They did not let the first obstacle deter them. They worked on the problem. Maybe they knew whose house it was, the Bible did not say; however, they were not concerned with the repercussions of their actions. Because they were daring, their friend met Jesus and became victorious over his issues. Now I am not telling you to go get your friends and drop them through the roof of your nearest church. I am telling you, though, be bold in your attempt to get your friends who need Jesus to Jesus.

Just like the SAS, Christians should live up to the motto of "Who dares wins." Be daring in your personal relationship with Jesus. No matter what is going on in the world around you, make your way to him. Boldly bring your issues and struggles to him, because he cares about you. Also be daring for your friends, family, and the world around you who need Jesus. Don't let an obstacle stop you from bringing them to Jesus. Boldly and bravely work the problem, always believing that victory is found only in Jesus.

Now if you are struggling with living a daring life, then check out these stories in the Bible of people who were daring for the Lord. You can learn about Moses in the entire book of Exodus. Rahab is a great example of not letting your past stop you from doing the right thing (Josh. 2). Daniel in the lion's den (Dan. 6), and Shadrach, Meshach, and Abednego (Dan.

3) show us how to be daring to serve the Lord when others tell us not to. Above anything, take some time and pray. Ask God to show you how to live a more daring life for him. Just like 1 Corinthians 16:13 tells us to stand firm, be courageous and strong.

"Be strong, and let your heart take courage, all you who wait for the Lord!" (Ps. 31:24 ESV).

9

Passion Makes Life Interesting

Then Jesus told his disciples, "If anyone would come after me,
let him deny himself and take up his cross and follow me."

—Matthew 16:34 (ESV)

I love quotes. I think quotes and motivational sayings are some
of the best forms of encouragement. They are also great tools
to inspire us. Athletic teams and businesses do this by post-
ing inspirational sayings or their core values around their facility. I have different quotes and maxims posted all around my
classroom for my students. They rage anywhere from "chess
not checkers" to "You can't be half a gangster" (that may be
my second book). Sometimes the right quote can be more
than encouraging. It can take you back to a story or an event
that impacted your life. For example, this quote: "Somewhere
inside, we hear a voice. It leads us in the direction of the person
we wish to become. But it's up to us whether or not to follow."
This is a quote from the late Pat Tillman. Now if you are like
me, when you read that, it gets your heart pumping or the hairs
on your arm stand up. For this chapter, we will use some of

Pat's quotes and the story of his life, and draw connections to our journey of discipleship.

You can read a more detailed biography on Pat on his foundation's website (pattillmanfoundation.org). I just want to give you a shorter version if you have never heard of him. Pat was born in California in 1976. During his time in school, he was described as a natural leader. In high school, he was a star on the football field. He was told he was too small to play at the collegiate level. However, Arizona State University saw something in Pat and offered him a scholarship. He was a three-time member of the PAC 10 All-Academic football team. After college, the Arizona Cardinals selected Pat in the seventh round of the 1998 draft. His determination helped him break the team record for tackles in the 2000 season. Pat also volunteered with different groups during the off season.

We know that on September 11, 2001, the world changed forever. After the events of that day, these are the words Pat told a reporter: "At times like this you stop and think about just how good we have it, what kind of system we live in, and the freedoms we are allowed. A lot of my family has gone and fought in wars and I really haven't done a damn thing." After this, in the spring of 2002, Pat married the love of his life. He then did something that would seem crazy to the majority of people today. Pat informed the Cardinals that he was placing his career on hold to join the military. To make the decision to walk away from the limelight and the millions of dollars shocked many people. You may be thinking this guy is crazy. There is no way I would walk away from that. Well, you would not be alone in that line of thought, but Pat had another path to follow.

Pat and his brother enlisted in the US Army. After going through basic training, they went to Ranger School. Once they completed that they were assigned to Seventy-fifth Ranger Regiment. A quick google search will give you an answer like this to the question: what is the difference between Army Rangers and Green Berets? Green Berets are the US Army's unconventional warfare unit, with specialty in search and rescue, peace keeping missions, and psychological warfare. Rangers are an elite light infantry unit that specializes in direct action raids, airfield seizure, and reconnaissance. So Rangers are elite in what they do. A buddy who served in the special operations community told me that there is no better group in the world to take and secure an airfield than the Army Rangers. This is the group that Pat was a part of.

During his time in the army, Pat served in both Iraq and Afghanistan. On the night of April 22, 2004, Pat's unit was ambushed while in a canyon in Afghanistan. Pat attempted to give cover fire to his brothers as they tried to escape the canyon. This led to Pat's death via fratricide or friendly fire. Although Pat is gone his friends and family started the Pat Tillman Foundation. I encourage you to take some time and go check out the work they are doing to carry on Pat's legacy.

My hope is that these connections for this chapter will inspire you to be a better disciple of Jesus. For this chapter, let's look at two of Pat's quotes. The first one is the one from Pat to introduce the chapter. *"Somewhere inside, we hear a voice. It leads us in the direction of the person we wish to become. But it's up to us whether or not to follow."* As Christians this question is part of the foundation of following Jesus. When we hear the Holy Spirit knocking on the door of our heart, will we let him in? Or you can think of it this way: will you follow Jesus when he calls you? How you answer that question determines the trajectory of your life.

In Matthew 4:18–22 we see Jesus calling his first disciples. This is after he went into the wilderness and was tempted by the devil. When he comes out of the wilderness, he begins his public ministry preaching this message in Matthew 4:17: "From that time on Jesus began to preach, "Repent, for the kingdom of heaven has come near" (NIV). This foundation would have been considered radical by people of that day. That brings us to our main passage in Matthew 4:18–22 where Jesus calls his first disciples:

> While walking by the Sea of Galilee, he saw two brothers, Simon (who is called Peter) and Andrew his brother, casting a net into the sea, for they were fishermen. And he said to them, "Follow me, and I will make you fishers of men." Immediately they left their nets and followed him. And going on from there he saw two other brothers, James the son of Zebedee and John his brother, in the boat with Zebedee their father, mending their nets, and he called them. Immediately they left the boat and their father and followed him. (ESV)

Let's look at some truths we can learn from text. The first is Jesus sees you where you are. The disciples did not have to clean up their life for Jesus to notice them. Jesus did not call them after they had fasted for a certain amount of time. Nor did he call them once they had cleaned up the sin in their life. No, he called them right in the middle of their life. So many people think that cleaning up their life is a requirement for following Jesus. Just like he called the first disciples, he calls us the same way, right in the middle of our life. Sometimes, Jesus calls you in the middle of the third verse of Amazing Grace during Sunday morning church. Sometimes he calls when you are out in the wilderness, or driving down the road. Sometimes it's right as your life is falling apart. No matter when it is, God calls you right where you are. It's up to us to choose if we will answer and follow God's call.

The second truth we can take away from the text is that Jesus knows you. Not only does he know your past, but he knows the plan God has for you. That plan is an invitation to be a part of his story ("*the* story") for his glory. We see this in his words to the disciples. Their identity was fishermen. That's who they were. Jesus tells them to follow me and I'll make you fishers of men. By taking the first step of following Jesus they took their first step in the mission they were created for. The God of all creation is calling you into a plan he designed specifically for you. If we want to walk in the path God has for us, then we must follow hard after Jesus. Even when you can't see the path, we follow hard after him. Because we trust and know that Jesus will lead us to the father. Following Jesus will always lead to a better situation than where the world has taken you. So do you want to be where the father is? If yes, then follow Jesus with everything we have.

The third truth from the scripture we need to look at is that our response is important. As soon as they heard Jesus say follow me, they dropped what they were doing and followed him. They did not wait or try to get prepared, they just followed. We need to have this same attitude in our lives. It is easy to create excuses to prolong the first step toward Jesus. Maybe some of these will sound familiar. "I need to stop drinking before I follow Jesus," or "I need to stop looking at pornography before I surrender my life to Jesus." Whatever the excuse is or how good it sounds at the end of the day it is an excuse! The truth is the only thing standing between us and Jesus is air and opportunity. Jesus does not give us a complex invitation, and because of that he does not require a complex response. His call does warrant a response, though, and that response should be made with a sense of urgency. One of the results of sin is that everyone dies.

So from the moment we are born, the sand is running out of the hourglass of our life. When our sand runs out, we don't get another chance to accept Jesus as Lord and Savior. If we don't accept his invitation of salvation in this life, we will forever be separated from him in eternity.

Psalm 118:24 says this: "This is the day that the Lord has made; let us rejoice and be glad in it" (ESV). That is true for us today. The Lord has made this day for me and you. We can rejoice because God is calling for us to follow him today. The God of creation, the maker of heaven and Earth, is calling us to go with him on this journey toward his glory. So if you have accepted Jesus as your Lord and Savior, then take a second and worship him for calling you out of sin and darkness and into the light of his glory. If you have never accepted that invitation, then get excited because today is your day! God wants to save you today! All you have to do is respond. Admit that you are a sinner and that sin separates you from him. Believe that Jesus came and lived a perfect life and paid the price of our sin with his death on the cross. Believe that he did what we could not do and conquer death by rising from the grave! Then finally confess Jesus is the savior and Lord of your life, and follow after him! Remember the path of our journey toward elite faith starts with the first step.

We can learn another lesson from one of Pat's quotes. This specific quote is one of my all-time favorites.

> Passion is what makes life interesting, what ignites our soul, fuels our love and carries our friendships, stimulates our intellect, and pushes our limits… A passion for life is contagious and uplifting. Passion cuts both ways… Those that make you feel on top of the world are equally able to turn it upside down… In

my life I want to create passion in my own life and with those I care for. I want to feel, experience and live every emotion. I will suffer through the bad for the heights of the good.

I believe that these were not just empty words. Pat Tillman lived these words out. Ever since I have heard this quote it gets my heart pumping. The connection I want to draw from it to the gospel makes me want to run through a wall for Jesus! It is simply this; when we see the greatness and glory of Jesus then the passion of our life becomes his renown. It ignites our soul, fuels our love, and pushes the limitations we put on ourselves. Or simply, it changes us.

Isaiah chapter 6 shows us the impact of seeing the Lord in all his glory can have on our life.

> In the year that King Uzziah died, I saw the Lord, high and exalted, seated on a throne; and the train of his robe filled the temple. Above him were seraphim, each with six wings: With two wings they covered their faces, with two they covered their feet, and with two they were flying. And they were calling to one another:
>
> "Holy, holy, holy is the Lord Almighty;
> the whole earth is full of his glory."
>
> At the sound of their voices the doorposts and thresholds shook and the temple was filled with smoke.
>
> "Woe to me!" I cried. "I am ruined! For I am a man of unclean lips, and I live among a people of unclean lips, and my eyes have seen the King, the Lord Almighty."

Then one of the seraphim flew to me with a live coal in his hand, which he had taken with tongs from the altar. With it he touched my mouth and said, "See, this has touched your lips; your guilt is taken away and your sin atoned for."

Then I heard the voice of the Lord saying, "Whom shall I send? And who will go for us?"

And I said, "Here am I. Send me!" (Isa. 6:1–8, NIV)

We can learn so many things from this small piece of scripture. Entire books could be written on just these few verses. For our journey in this book let's just look at a few. Understand that in Isaiah chapters 1 through 5, we see God laying out the problem with how the people had rebelled against the covenant between his people and himself. Isaiah was the mouthpiece for God to the people. Then in chapter 6, Isaiah sees the Lord. Now we know from the scripture that this vision was like nothing Isaiah or anyone of us has ever seen. Not only does he see how great the Lord is, he sees the train of his robe filling the temple. Not only does he see how mighty the Lord is, he hears the sound of the worship to him shaking the foundations of the temple. The most important thing that Isaiah sees is how holy God is. *Merriam-Webster* defines holy as this: "exalted or worthy of complete devotion as one perfect in goodness and righteousness." I pray that we can see the holiness of God today because when we see it, there is an instant changing impact in our life. Look at the effect it had on Isaiah. When he sees just how holy God is, he realizes just how corrupt he and his generation are.

God sits on a throne that only he could occupy. God has no rival or equal. He is also always good. We can be good some of the time or most of the time but we can also be bad. God on the other hand is always good. When Isaiah realizes this, it brings him to a state of shame and guilt. The same is true for us. When we realize just how good and holy God is, we know that there is no possible way we can measure up. On our own, we have no hope and we don't deserve to be in the presence of holy God. Just like Isaiah, though, God does not leave us in that place. God sent Jesus to take our guilt and atone for our sin by way of the cross. We can put our faith and trust in him because he is holy. God will never sin against us. He will always be exactly who he says he is. He will never let us down.

So God is worthy of all the praise we can bring him because of who he is. Isaiah saw that, and I hope today you can too. I hope that we can never take for granted who God is, or how blessed we are to be able to come into his presence. I hope we never forget how awesome it is to be able to bring our problems and praise to God, and how crazy it is that he cares about us. That is what our passion must be made of!

The second thing I want to draw your attention to is Isaiah's response to God's question. When God asks, "Who can I send?" Without hesitation Isaiah says, "Here I am, send me." After seeing the greatness and goodness of God he does not shy away from the task that God has. He does not make excuses for why God can't use him. He jumps at the opportunity and says I am right here God, send me. That is something we all need to do. God's work is not done. He wants us to be a part of taking the good news of Jesus to the ends of the Earth. So the question is, will we make that mission the passion of our life. Will we take the gospel to our family and friends? Will we share Jesus with our coworkers and city? That passion for God will make your life interesting. That passion for Jesus will also push our limits. The things we think that we can't do, God will show us, with him, we can. Moses thought there was no way he could lead God's people out of bondage in Egypt. Not with what he had done in the past. But God says it's not you, it's me working through you. The question for us is will I say yes to what God wants to do? Will the response of our life be "Here I am, send me"?

If we want to be an asset for the Lord, we must have the "Here I am, send me" attitude. We also need a radical passion for the one true, holy God. That passion for God will fuel our love, push our limits, and carry our friendships. I don't know about you but I know I need more of that. I know I can be a better husband, father, teacher, coach, and friend if my heart is full of a pure and holy passion for Jesus. What parts of you could benefit from a heart full of passion for Jesus? If the answer is yes, there are parts of me that could use more Jesus, then take some time and pray and ask God to fill you up. The more we meet with God the more our cup will be overflowing. So make it a priority to meet with God. Not only for yourself but for the ones around you also.

As we close this chapter, I would like to take a second and pray for you and for me. We are not on this journey alone.

Father,

> We love you! You are holy, holy, holy. You have no rival or equal. We don't deserve your love and mercy and grace. Thank you for sending Jesus to make a way for us God. Thank you, Jesus, for taking our guilt and shame by way of the cross and being the atonement for our sin. Fill us right now with the holy spirit and a never-ending passion for you. Help us show that passion in every area of our lives. Let our answer to you always be

"Here I am, send me." For you alone are God, and you alone are worthy of all the glory, honor, and praise. We love you God and we ask all of these things in Jesus's name, amen.

A passion for Jesus will never lead to a dull boring life. No, it will always make life interesting, amazing journey.

10

Not According to Plan

And we know that for those who love God all things work together for good, for those who are called according to his purpose.

—Romans 8:28 (ESV)

In the early 1990s, the country of Somalia was experiencing a famine of biblical proportions. This occurred because of a few reasons. Drought in the 1970s was one issue. War-torn governments and different clans were creating more problems than solutions. Those clans were using hunger as a weapon against their own people. So between the civil war and drought, the country of Somalia was in a tough spot. During this time, over 300,000 Somalians died of starvation.

The United Nations (UN) peacekeeping efforts had a hard time restoring order to the country. In 1992, then president George H. Bush sent in Marines to Mogadishu as part of the mission "Operation Restore Hope." The death of twenty-four UN soldiers warranted the arrest of Mohamed Farrah Aidid. He was the leader of one of the worst clans in Mogadishu. This led to the events of October 3, 1993, which many people know as "Black Hawk Down."

On that day the US attempted a capture mission of two of Aidid's higher ranking leaders. The mission was known as "Operation Gothic Serpent" The objectives of the mission were simple. First Army Rangers and Delta force (Delta force is the army's counter terrorism unit in the special operations world) would chopper into the target building. Delta would execute the search and capture of the HVTs, while the rangers would fast rope down and hold a perimeter around the building. A group of Humvees and other vehicles would wait at a staging point to come in and take the HVT and delta and ranger elements back to base. The entire timeline of the mission should have taken less than an hour. There was already pressure on this mission because it was being conducted in the middle of the day. Ideally this would have been done at night. The military felt the reward outweighed the risk.

However, things did not go according to plan. At the beginning of the mission one of the rangers fell from the black hawk and had to be evacuated back to base. The convoy ran into problems with local militias setting up roadblocks. Those were not the only major problems the US forces encountered that day. Two black hawk helicopters were shot down by local militia. This led to the eighteen-hour firefight between delta operators and rangers who rushed to the rescue of the pilots, and crew. The aftermath of this operation left eighteen US soldiers and hundreds of Somalians dead.

Because of all the loss it would be hard to classify the operation as a success. We can, however, learn from the actions of different heroes that day when things did not go according to plan. The first example we will look at is the actions of Master Sergeant Gary Gordon, and Sergeant First Class Randell Shughart. When the second black hawk went down (Super

Six-Four), the ground elements were unable to assist the second crash site due to the engagement of local militia forces. Both men wanted to assist but their request was denied multiple times. Finally, however, they were granted permission to be inserted to assist the black hawk crew. Pilot Mike Duhrant was the only survivor of the crew that day. Gordon and Shughart fought their way to the crash site and attempted to defend it with only sniper rifles and pistols. Both men lost their lives that day. Both Gordon and Shughart men were awarded the Medal of Honor posthumously for their heroic actions They were also the first to receive the honor since the Vietnam war.

By the time they were inserted into the action, they understood how things had fallen apart. From the soldier that fell to two downed helicopters, this was about as far from the plan and you could get. However, seeing the need they asked to step right into the fire. After asking and being denied, they could have left alone. They could have told themselves, "Hey, we tried, so it's not on us." Gordon and Shughart kept asking. Not for the chance at glory, but because there was a need and they were able.

In our Christian life, will we ask God to insert us into the action? Where we see a need and know the gifts and skills God gave us could help. Are we praying to God, let me be a blessing to someone else? It's easy to ask God to insert you onto the mountain top, but will you ask to be inserted in the valley of the shadow of death? If we're honest, we look more like Ananias than Gordon and Shughart.

Now Ananias was only mentioned in the Bible twice, but because of his willingness to step into the plan God had for him he had a huge impact on the church and the spread of the gospel. We are first introduced to Ananias in Acts chapter 9. Before we are introduced to him, we find Saul threatening the followers of Jesus and doing everything he can to stop the early

Christian church. When Steven is stoned to death, Saul was there. On the road to Damascus, Saul has an encounter with Jesus that changed his life. The Bible tells us in Acts 9 that that encounter left him blinded. The people with Saul led him to Damascus and for three days he was blind and did not eat or drink. Then in steps Ananias.

> In Damascus there was a disciple named Ananias. The Lord called to him in a vision, "Ananias!"
>
> "Yes, Lord," he answered.
>
> The Lord told him, "Go to the house of Judas on Straight Street and ask for a man from Tarsus named Saul, for he is praying. In a vision he has seen a man named Ananias come and place his hands on him to restore his sight."
>
> "Lord," Ananias answered, "I have heard many reports about this man and all the harm he has done to your holy people in Jerusalem. And he has come here with authority from the chief priests to arrest all who call on your name."
>
> But the Lord said to Ananias, "Go! This man is my chosen instrument to proclaim my name to the Gentiles and their kings and to the people of Israel. I will show him how much he must suffer for my name."
>
> Then Ananias went to the house and entered it. Placing his hands on Saul, he said, "Brother Saul, the Lord—Jesus, who appeared to you on the road as you were coming here—has sent me so that you may

see again and be filled with the Holy Spirit." Immediately, something like scales fell from Saul's eyes, and he could see again. He got up and was baptized, and after taking some food, he regained his strength. (Acts 9:10–19 NIV)

Now we know from the scripture that he was a disciple or follower of Jesus. His response to God asking him to do something was interesting. He does what many of us would do, he questions God. Ananias said are you sure God? I have heard that Saul is a bad dude coming after your church. Are you sure you want me to help him? Now it's easy to sit and think who is this guy to question God. If we search our own heart, though, we will find that our answer often sounds a lot like Ananias. We like to tell ourselves that we would be like Gordon and Shugart. When they saw a need, they asked the command to be inserted to assist with the problem. We would like to tell ourselves that our response would be the same. However, more and more our responses and actions sound like Ananias.

Ananias could not see how God was going to use Saul. All he saw was what he knew. I don't blame him at all. Honestly, I would more than likely do the same thing. I would also probably be like James and John (the sons of thunder) and ask God to rain down fire on someone. If you are like me, you have had that same conversation with God. It sounds something like this; God how does this person do all the wrong things and still life works out for them? Although that is our nature to want justice it is not our spirit when we are in Christ Jesus. When Jesus is our Lord and Savior, we have a new spirit, the Holy Spirit, living in us!

We live in a world today with over three billion people who are unreached. Many simply have no access or have not been told the good news of Jesus. Most of them are experiencing physical needs as well as spiritual. None of that takes into account the unreached and physical needs of our community. While they have access to the gospel, they don't know Jesus as Lord and Savior. While no one single church or person can win the war against the hungry, homeless, and victims of the world alone. The church and the individual can be an asset in the battle. Let's look at some different ways to be inserted into the battle.

First, a quick Google search can bring you to the stat that in 2020, 25 percent of children lived in a single-parent home. That makes sense, although it is reported (www.fatherly.com) the divorce rate in America is the lowest since the 1970s, there are still families breaking up every year. When that happens most of the time the kids become collateral damage. You may be thinking how can I help with that problem? We may not be able to fix marriages and restore families, but we can make a difference in a kid's life. Volunteering to lead a youth small group and work the nursery at church can make a huge impact. Although you can't be with them 24-7, you can show them Jesus by the way you love and care about them in the time you have.

Maybe instead of helping with the kids you start a food pantry in your church to feed the hungry. The old saying is "Give a man a fish, he eats for a day. Teach a man to fish and he eats for life." Although that is true, it is hard to learn when you're hungry. So giving someone one meal will not solve the hunger problem forever, but it will fill an instant need and create an opportunity to share the gospel.

God has blessed you with skills and talents to be an asset in your world today. We can lean in and trust what Romans 8:28 that things will work out for those who are called to God's purpose. Don't fool yourself either. God did not give you the talents and platform and reach to only live for your purpose. We are created and called to be a part of God's story, for his plan and his purpose. So today take some time and ask God to prepare your heart to be inserted into the action, and like Gordon and Shughart ask God to insert you into the action. Just like Ananias, though we may only directly impact one person, but that one person (just like Saul who became Paul and wrote most of the New Testament) can impact the entire world.

Ask God to open your eyes to see the need around you. During the early 1800s, Harriet Beecher Stowe wrote a book called *Uncle Tom's Cabin.* The book shined a light on the cruelty of slavery in the south. Although slavery had been going on for years, it was not until people read her book that their eyes were open to the horrors and hardship African American slaves faced. Abraham Lincoln made this comment about Stowe, he called her "the little woman who wrote the book that started this great war." Sometimes all it takes is seeing the problem to know that you can and should help. Ask God to see the world how he sees it.

Another example from the battle of Mogadishu is from Major Jeff Struecker. I first heard of Major Struecker in a sermon from Ben Stuart at Passion 2022. This led me to research him and find out more of his story. I found his website (jeffstrucker.com) where I got to hear his account of the events that day from a speech he gave at Liberty University. Struecker was the driver of the Humvee where the first casualty that day took place. A soldier was shot while en route back to base. Major Struecker describes that when they got back to base before they went back into the city someone told him to clean the blood out of the Humvee. They said it would cause mental problems to the men who had to sit in another soldier's blood. As he took rags and buckets of water, he said the fear that this could be his blood struck him. Major Struecker said he did what any good

Christian would do and he prayed. He said it was after that that he found peace that only Jesus could give in this truth. The truth was this: if he died that day, he would be with Jesus, and if he lived, he would go home to be with his wife and child. After that, Major Struecker said he was calm all throughout the night as they went back and forth, carrying men to and from the battle. The next morning, he says that a lot of soldiers asked him how he stayed so calm in all of the chaos that night. He got to share with them about Jesus, and found a new purpose for his life. Major Struecker became an Army Chaplain for the same unit he served in.

Major Struecker's story is a real-life example of Romans 8:28: "And we know that for those who love God all things work together for good, for those who are called according to his purpose" (ESV). Even though Operation Gothic Serpent went sideways, God used it for his good and purpose. Sometimes we think that good means everyone makes it, or everyone gets a happy ending. Sadly, that is not the world that we live in. Paul, however, tells us in his letter to the church at Philippi that regardless of his outcome he will glorify God. Philippians 1:21, "For to me to live is Christ, and to die is gain" (ESV). For the reader of the letter, this was a huge statement because they knew Paul was writing this while in prison, likely facing death. This is a truth that we can lean on when things don't go according to our plan. No matter if the outcome is good or bad, we know that in the end we will be with Jesus. So if we go home to be with him, hallelujah! If we stay here on Earth, we get to keep operating in the mission Jesus gave us.

The last connection I want to draw from the Black Hawk Down story is the action of the army while searching for Mike Duhrant. Although he was taken prisoner and in a bad spot the army and his unit let him know they would not leave him behind. As they flew over the city, they blared messages saying,

"We will not leave without you." Now I can't speak for him, but that had to bring some comfort to know they had not forgotten him.

As Christians, we should be doing the same thing. In our world it is more common to come across people whose lives have not, not gone according to plan. Whatever the cause (cancer, job loss, COVID, divorce, addiction) what every person wants to know is does anyone care? Does anyone see me living in this struggle? This is where Christians must step in. We know that there are some problems we can't fix. We can't cure cancer or fix marriages. As bad as we want to, sometimes the solution is outside our control. What we can do is love them through it. We can let people know we are not going to leave them in the mess. In every step out of the valley, back to the mountaintop, we will be there.

My favorite superhero is Captain America (go figure, right?). If you don't know a lot about Cap, his best friend is Bucky Barnes. The arch of their story takes them in two different directions. Even when it looks like Bucky is completely bad and has no hope, Cap tells him, "I am with you to the end of the line." That is what our outreach strategy as a church should be, because it was Jesus's strategy. He did not say come to this event, or come to this meeting every week. No, he said, "Follow me." We should follow him because he told us he will be with us to the end of the line. "Teaching them to observe all that I have commanded you. And behold, I am with you always, to the end of the age" (Matt. 28:20 ESV).

Mike Tyson famously said, "Everyone has a plan until they get punched in the mouth." I have found that that is true in life. Your response after you get hit in the mouth is more important than what caused the punch. When I was in college, a buddy of mine got into an altercation after a football game. Our team had gotten beat and he had too many adult beverages during the game. So he was mad, and he was drunk (that's never a good combination). He then looks at me and a few other guys and says let's go get in a fight. Now we laugh at him and tell him to sober up and calm down. See we had wristbands to get into a big party that night. Sadly, we never made it. One of our buddies (in his drunkenness) thought that sounded like a good idea. So off they go into the quad looking for trouble. Anytime you go looking for trouble you will usually find more than you wanted. I told one of our friends standing with me that we might want to grab them, but by then it was too late. They decided to pick a fight with the biggest guy he could find. It was not a long altercation; it was a classic, though. One friend took a jab straight to the mouth bending his front teeth back at a 45-degree angle, and his buddy (who thought it was a good idea to go pick a fight) got a power bomb, though, a tailgate tent for his troubles. So after this altercation, we had to call his parents because he got his teeth literally knocked backward. Our night was over before it began. When his mom and dad got to his apartment (a two-hour drive) they were pretty ticked. His dad looked at me and asked Drew, what should he have done differently in this situation. In my brilliance and sarcasm, I said the first thing that came to my mind…. I told him he should have ducked. I don't think he spoke to me the rest of the night. No matter what advice I gave he still got punched in the face. We may not all get decked in the middle of the quad after a game, but life will punch us in the mouth and change our plans. I hope that through this chapter you can find encouragement to lean in and trust God's ultimate plan for our life.

If you are struggling with that trust, or maybe your life feels like it has gone off the rails lately, check out these passages from scripture, and ask God to help you fill your heart with trust in him and his plan.

Proverbs 3:5–6, John 3:16, Psalm 94:14, Hebrews 13:6, 2 Timothy 1:7, John 14:18.

"Everyone has a plan until they get punched in the mouth" (Mike Tyson).

The Battle May Be over, but the War Rages On

For the weapons of our warfare are not of the flesh
but have divine power to destroy strongholds.

—2 Corinthians 10:4

What goes on outside the wire causes collateral damage that war fighters can't leave on the battlefield. Physical injuries and the chance of losing one's life have been a part of war ever since people started fighting each other. However, the mental injuries have been long overlooked. The saying "War is hell" does not do it justice. Soldiers can take the uniform off, and put their gun down, but the problem is they cannot forget what they have seen, or what they have done. They bring all of that mental and emotional baggage back inside the wire. That is a battle they can fight for years.

How do you unsee kids carrying around guns? A bullet from gun is the same no matter who pulls the trigger. How do you unsee women wearing suicide vest, and being used as a weapon? How do you block out losing a buddy who was fighting right beside you? I had a veteran tell me that until you have pulled that trigger with your sight on another human you have no idea what war is like. He was 100 percent right. I have no idea what war is like. The vast majority of the world does not know what war is like. No matter how many books we read or movies we watch we will never truly understand.

Every battle wound is not visible, but left untreated it can be life threatening. Veterans coming home are dealing with wounds they can't see. Sometimes they don't even know they are there. One of the issues that veterans face when returning from war is post-traumatic stress disorder (PTSD). Another is traumatic brain injuries (TBI). Because of this and other issues we are losing veterans at an alarming rate. The Military Veteran Project reports that an average of twenty-two veterans a day commit suicide. When I heard that statistic it punched me right in the gut! Because every one of those twenty-two are someone's family member. I don't believe that God makes mistakes. I believe that he has a plan and a purpose for everyone. This is a vital truth that everyone must cling to when the devil tries to whisper lies in our ear. When we feel worthless and broken, we must run to John 3:16. That truth that God loves us so much he gave his son for us has to become our strong tower against the lies of the enemy. When the devil says nobody cares, God says you are loved. The only opinion about us that we should ever care about is God's. He is the maker and ruler of the universe. He is the beginning and end. So what he thinks about you is all that matters.

Before we look at what God thinks about you, let's look at some of the wounds that veterans deal with. Some of this will resonate with you even if you have never served in the military. Soldiers are not the only ones who can struggle with PTSD or TBI. I will try my best to explain the effects of both. Before I get into this, I want you to understand that I am not trying to shame you if you suffer from something we are going to discuss. I want to do the opposite! I want to encourage you. I want to shine a light on the glory of God and point you to him. I know that in Jesus and with help you can find peace. Jesus tells us this in Matthew 11:28: "Come to me, all you who are weary and burdened, and I will give you rest" (NIV). We know that Jesus is not a liar, so if he tells us that he will give us rest then we can take it to the bank that he will. Remember everything is in his time. Trust that he will walk you out of the valley and lead you beside still water.

The American Psychiatric Association defines PTSD like this: "a psychiatric disorder that may occur in people who have experienced or witnessed a traumatic event such as a natural disaster, a serious accident, a terrorist act, war/combat, or rape or who have been threatened with death, sexual violence or serious injury." This problem also used to be known as "shell shock" or "combat fatigue." However, PTSD is not limited to people who saw combat. It can also be caused by prolonged exposure to traumatic events. Any type of traumatic event can cause problems for the individual. They can experience flash-backs or nightmares. The US Department of Veteran Affairs lists that between eleven to twenty out of every one hundred soldiers who were involved in Operation Enduring Freedom or Operation Iraqi Freedom have PTSD in a given year. The added stress of what the soldier did in the war or the politics surround-ing the war can be factors that lead to PTSD. The American Psychiatric Association lists some of the symptoms of PTSD as intrusive thoughts or flashbacks of the event; avoiding people, places, events that may trigger distressing memories; alterations in mental cognition or mood of a person. Anger outburst or reckless behavior can be other symptoms of PTSD as well. The Department of Veteran Affairs says that about six out of every one hundred people will have PTSD at some point in their life.

The Center of Disease Control describes a TBI as "a disruption in the normal function of the brain that can be caused by a bump, blow, or jolt to the head, or penetrating head injury." The Defense and Veterans Brain Injury Center reported 414,000 TBIs among US service members between the year 2000–2019 (basically the war on terror). More than 185,000 veterans have been diagnosed with a TBI. Conditions from TBI can be headaches, sleep disorders, memory problems, slower thinking, and depression. These can lead to long term mental and physical problems. As well as create issues that impact families, relationships, employment just to name a few.

Major strides have been made by the government in the mental care of veterans. Veterans have more access to helpful services today than ever before. The progress that has been made over the past few decades is encouraging. So much time and resources are spent on teaching these soldiers how to be proficient war fighters, while not much is invested into helping them deal with the effects of war fighting. It is a tough balance for the government to be mission minded and try to win the war, while also focusing on the wellbeing of the soldiers who complete those missions. The military operates under the motto "No man left behind," and we as Christians and civilians should operate under that same motto inside the wire. No matter the trauma we don't leave people behind.

The same can be said about people in the civilian world. So many people today struggle with PTSD or TBI. No matter if it was combat that caused the injury, or something else the effects are the same. There is truth in the saying that first step to healing is admitting there is a problem. Whether it be veterans or civilians there is a stigma out there that if you need mental help then you're crazy. That can't be further from the truth. Until you address the problem you can't work the problem. You are not alone in this struggle. Many people struggle with mental health every single day. The old saying goes be kind to everyone because you never know what hell they are walking through. I have found that to be 100 percent true. Let me give you an example. One day in one of my classes we had a lot of students out. So I began to just talk to the few students about the plan for that class period, when the students cut me off and started to talk about life. They began to open up about everything they have going on in their life. Sixth period history quickly turned into a therapy session. They had been holding back all of the stress and pain and for whatever reason the dam broke that day and all of those emotions and feelings rushed out. The things they told me they are struggling with broke my heart. They talked about the loss of family members, to having to work to pay for their bills, and to coming out to their parents with their sexuality. Just like them, so many people are walking around every day, wanting to open up and talk about the struggles they face in their life, but can't figure out where to turn. Please understand we don't have to agree with everything they do or their life decisions. It is not our job to be the judge of their life. We are called to love our neighbor as ourselves. That is the role we play in others' healing journeys.

If you are the one walking through the darkest valley of your life, I want to encourage you. There is hope! You were not made to stay in the valley. Admitting there is a problem does not make you weak. The attitude of "just suck it up" will only cover up the problem, just like how a bandage can stop the bleeding from a gunshot wound, but you still want to go to the hospital and get that checked out. Using the just suck it up mentality acts like bandage. It can help you get through the moment, but it does not fix the problem. If you are in a position to show the love of Jesus to someone hurting, do it! We are called by the King to be his witnesses to the end of the Earth. Don't forget that call is a charge to tell the world about God's amazing grace, and unfathomable mercy.

Life gives us hard things to handle, whether it be our own issues or our neighbors. No matter how hard it is, though, I want to encourage you to take heart because our hope is found in our access to the savior. A savior who does not push you away or cast you out because of your brokenness. He does the opposite; he calls you to him with his arms wide open. Romans 8:34 tells us that Jesus is interceding for us right now to God the father: "Who is to condemn? Christ Jesus is the one who died—more than that, who was raised—who is at the right hand of God, who indeed is interceding for us" (ESV). He is like the dad in Jesus's parable of the prodigal son (Luke 15:11–32). When the dad hears he is coming from all the sin and shame of his bad decisions, He takes off running to meet him. This is what Jesus does for us.

I want to show some different examples of how Jesus interacted with people the world thought was broken. My hope is that through them you can see just how much Jesus cares about you and what you are going through. That it would be an encouragement that would push you to the father, not pull you away. I encourage you to go to the word and read these encounters for yourself.

The first example is from John chapter 5:1–15. Here we find Jesus in Jerusalem, and while there, he goes to a place called Bethesda. There was a pool there and people believed that when the water was stirred it had healing power if you could be the first one into it. This is a place where many sick or hurt people would have come to. Hoping for a miracle. Jesus finds a man who had been crippled for nearly forty years. He had been at the pool a long time and never made it into the water. Someone would always beat him to it. Jesus goes right up to him and asks him if he wants to be healed. I think it's interesting that Jesus goes up to him. He could have healed anyone at the pool (there were options), but yet he goes up to this man. One who had been broken for a long time, and thought no one cared. Jesus told him to get up and at once for the first time in decades the man got up and walked. How awesome is it that Jesus heals the one who had run out of hope? The encouragement we can take from this is that just like the man at the pool Jesus sees us, and cares enough to insert himself in our situation. He is not a savior who turns his head from our pain. He is a savior who takes our pain and places it on himself.

The second example, we will look at is found in Mark 1:40–45. Jesus is met by a leper who falls at his feet. Jesus not only lets him near him, but he has pity, reaches out and touches him and heals him. There we can see two key truths for us to hold on to. The first is that Jesus did not tell the leper to get back. People during this time would want to stay a certain distance from them because of fear they would catch the disease. So the leper comes and falls at Jesus's feet and is not driven away. No matter how broken the world says we are, we can come fall at the feet of the King of kings. The second truth is that not only did Jesus let him close, but he touched him. This would have been a big no-no as he was seen as unclean. Jesus did not care what the world thought, though, because he had pity for this man and what he was going through. He does the same for us, reaching out for us and promising to never let us go. No matter if no one understands what you have gone through and the pain and issues it has caused, Jesus cares for you. You can fall at his feet anytime and bring your worry and burden to him. We have a savior who does not push us away!

The final example we will look at is found in Matthew 4:18–22. This is where Jesus calls the first disciples. He walks by the sea and finds Peter and his brother Andrew fishing. That was their job and livelihood. Jesus does something interesting, he says follow me and I will make you fishers of men. So Jesus invites them into a new purpose with him. He called them right then, though. He did not say go get ready, get your prayer life right and giving right and then follow me. No right there in that moment he says follow me just as you are. The same is true for us. No matter what we are going through, Jesus is calling us to follow him just as we are. We don't have to clean our life up to follow Jesus. When you follow Jesus, you will clean your life up willingly. Because the more time you spend with Jesus, the more you want to be like him. Even more than that, the more you want your life to make him proud.

These are only a few examples of how Jesus dealt with what the world classified as the outcast and the broken. Understand God is not scared of our problems. He is not caught off guard if we bring him our issues. God is the creator of the heavens and Earth, so we can trust our problems are not too big for him. I don't know what you are walking through, but I do want to encourage you that if you struggle with PTSD or symptoms from a TBI or any mental issue, reach out and get help. You are fearfully and wonderfully made and God has a plan for your life. Or if you know someone dealing with either of the above mentioned be the hands and feet of Jesus. We don't have to have the right answers or the perfect words to say; we just have to be willing to listen and show the love that God shows us. I want to leave you with this reminder. Remember when Shadrach, Meshach, and Abednego were thrown into the fire, God did not leave them alone. He was right there in the fire with them! Our God does not leave us alone in the fire.

If you are struggling today with some of these issues, reach out and get help. I want to point you to the gospels. The first step should always be with Jesus, so go through Matthew, Mark, Luke, and John and see just how much Jesus cares for the broken. I also want you to know that I am praying for everyone who reads this that is struggling. Know someone cares and has prayed for you.

After-Action Report

Growth comes from getting out of your comfort zone and stepping into the unknown. We see this in the scripture when Peter walks on water.

> And Peter answered him, "Lord, if it is you, command me to come to you on the water." He said, "Come." So Peter got out of the boat and walked on the water and came to Jesus. But when he saw the wind, he was afraid, and beginning to sink he cried out, "Lord, save me." Jesus immediately reached out his hand and took hold of him, saying to him, "O you of little faith, why did you doubt?" (Matt. 14:28–31 ESV)

It is uncomfortable to step into what God has placed on your heart. We walk into those moments with boldness and confidence. The pressure is not on you. If you fail (and you will because we all fail), Jesus is there to catch you.

Stepping into this project was very uncomfortable for me. If you put me in front of a crowd, I feel right at home. Writing, on the other hand, was never something I was great at. If you don't believe me, you can ask my former English teachers. I can say without a shadow of a doubt that I have grown through this process. Not because of anything that I have done but all because of what God has done. In my struggles and fear of not being good enough, God has been there to remind me that he can use anyone. No matter what faults or shortcomings we have, his grace and power can clear any personal hurdles we have.

God also showed me through his grace during this process that I was not okay. I was holding onto some emotional wounds that I didn't even know the impact those wounds were having on my life and my discipleship journey. Because of past experiences and what people had done to me I put up walls to defend my heart. While it kept me from getting hurt it also kept me from loving people how I should. Although I could feel the impact, I never addressed the issue. It was not till I heard it from someone who I had put walls up against that it made sense. I was wounded and had been acting from that wounded position for years. Always asking God to help me forgive the people who hurt me, but for whatever reason, I never asked him to heal those wounds. The Bible tells us to bring our wounds to Jesus because he can heal us of all our afflictions.

> Blessed be the God and Father of our Lord Jesus Christ, the Father of mercies and God of all comfort, who comforts us in all our affliction, so that we may be able to comfort those who are in any affliction, with the comfort with which we ourselves are comforted by God. For as we share abundantly in Christ's sufferings, so through Christ we share abundantly in comfort too. (2 Cor. 1:3–5 ESV)

By living with those wounds, it causes our discipleship trajectory to be arched. The shortest distance between two points is a straight line. Strive to make your discipleship journey a straight line from you to Jesus. Don't be like me and take the long way around. You could miss out on so many blessings from God.

One of the main things I have learned is to be dependent upon God's holy, perfect word. Every time when I would struggle with how do I make this make sense, and how do I take what's in my heart and put that on paper? God, through the Holy Spirit, would always take me back to the word. Above anything else that's what matters. The Word of God does not need my help. It can stand undefeated by itself. I hope that if I did nothing else in the book, that I pointed you to the truth of God's Word. If I did, I can count this as a mission accomplished.

Understand that mottos and stories can be great reminders and inspiration to us. It means nothing if we don't put in the work. If we want to be a better disciple for Jesus, then we have to put in the work. We have to make time to get into the word and learn about who God is and what he cares about. Finding time to pray and talk with God should never be something we only do one day a week. Or like Maverick in the movie *Top Gun* where he holds Goose's dog tags and says, "Talk to me, Goose" when he is nervous and scared. Our faith should not be something we keep in a glass case and only broken in case of emergencies. The Navy SEALS have a saying: "The more you bleed in training, the less you bleed in battle." Adopting that same mindset in our faith is for our benefit. The harder we work at our faith on the mountaintop, the stronger it will be in the valley.

Putting in the work is never easy. That's why it's called work. We have to find an excuse to do it. You can talk yourself out of anything hard. It's hard to make yourself do something challenging. I heard a BUDS instructor say on a documentary, "Find an excuse to win." Ever since then I have used that phrase with every team I have ever coached. It's just as relevant in life as it is in sports or special operations. We need to find an excuse to win in this battle of our faith. My excuse is my wife and daughters. With everything they went through I wanted to be someone they could count on. And to be someone who showed them Jesus day in and day out. That is my closest circle of influence. If I am an asset to the world but a liability to my family, then I have failed.

Part of AARs (After-Action Reports) is looking back on the mission and seeing what worked and what did not work. I am excited to tell you what I have seen God do during this part of my life. First, I have seen God take care of my wife every single day. To date all of her tests have been good and prognosis is promising. They even said with time they can permanently fix her vocal cord in time. She is excited for the time she can yell at me again (just kidding, Gena). With my daughter it's like watching God work a miracle every day. Through speech therapy we have seen her communication grow every week. I can't even begin to tell you how much I cried the first time she looked at me and said, "I love you, Daddy." I was not sure if I would ever hear her say those words. God deserves all glory and praise for all of her progress. He placed great people and therapists in her life with the skills to help her. Every daycare teacher she has had poured so much love into her. I am forever grateful to them and to God for all of it.

One of the things that I am most excited about is the AAR that you are going to have after this journey. I know God is good and is doing a great work in your life, and wants to do so much more in your life. When I think about the work God is doing, my heart and mind go to the lyrics of the worship song "Oceans" by Hillsong. I think the words beautifully describe this process. The words of the song are simply this: "Spirit lead me where my trust is without borders, Let me walk upon the waters, Wherever You would call me, Take me deeper than my feet could ever wander, And my faith will be made stronger, In the presence of my Saviour." We need to trust the Holy Spirit to lead us where our trust has no borders, and to go wherever he calls us. Part of being a tier 1 asset is going where you are needed.

I also have found wisdom in the SEAL saying: "Don't run to your death." We do have to run and follow after Jesus. We need to follow his example by getting away and spending time with God in prayer. When we do this, we can make sure our heart and motives are aligned with God's. I thought this would be like writing and preparing for a big sermon. I told a buddy it would take me a few weeks. I am thankful for his encouragement to take my time and make sure I get it right. The Bible teaches us this very lesson in Philippians 4:6: "Do not be anxious about anything, but in every situation, by prayer and petition, with thanksgiving, present your requests to God" (NIV). In whatever God is leading you to, make sure you walk through it by prayer and with thanksgiving. Be thankful the God of the heavens is using you in his story.

So as our journey comes to a close, I want to leave you with the motto of my favorite coach ever Nick Saban "the process." It's all about focusing and doing the things it takes to be good. That is what I hope and pray that all of us try to do every day. It means focusing on and working to become the best disciple of Jesus we can be. We must trust that the hard times we walk through is God molding and refining us into his image. Have faith in whatever God's process is for you, trusting that it is for your good and his glory.

I want you to know that you have been prayed for. I prayed that God will show you how great he is through this journey, just like he showed me! I pray that where you are struggling you will find God's perfect peace. I pray that the Holy Spirit inspires you and leads you wherever God calls you. I pray above everything, though, that if you do not know Jesus as your personal savior that you have seen just how much he loves you through the pages of this book. I ask that God do all these things for you and more in Jesus's holy name, amen!

Acknowledgments

This book covered a decade of research and lessons. Words do not do justice to all the people I need to thank. It takes a village and each of you plays a vital role in my journey.

Jesus. Above anyone, I want to thank you, Jesus, for never giving up on me. For always loving me. For showing me grace when I don't deserve it. Also for giving me this platform to take the passion inside of my heart and share it with the world.

Gena, you are my best friend. Thank you for walking through this journey with me. Thank you for always taking care of the girls and letting me go do what God has put on my heart! Never forget you are my hero and I love you forever and ever Amen.

Emory Kate and Sadie, I want you to know that I love you always, and I will forever strive to be someone you can be proud of.

Mom and Dad, thank you for everything. You are the best parents in the world, and I love you with all my heart. I would not be who I am today without you.

Tony, thank you for reading all these stories and making sure I get the military side of the book right. You have been a friend for a long-time brother, and I am thankful for you.

Leonard, Blake, Bryant, Seth, Adam, and Ron, thank you for reading this piece by piece and encouraging me to keep going with the book. You are all great men that I am proud to call my friends.

Donna Ingram and Amy Wagnon, thank you for proofing my book for me. You both are awesome, and I am so blessed to have had each of you as my teacher.

Daniel Barkley, thank you for looking over it and making sure I honored God with my connections to the scriptures.

To all of my students, you are forever an inspiration to me. Always remember rule no. 3: "Overuse *I love you.*"

You, thank you for reading my book. I hope you got as much out of this journey as I did.

Last but certainly not least, the special operations community: Your hard work, dedication, lessons, and stories were my inspiration for this book. Thank you for all the sacrifices you make for our freedom every day.

Notes

This is the list of all the resources I used for this book. I encourage you if you would like to know more about the special operations community, please check these sources out.

Chapter 1:

Basic Army Training, www.goarmy.com

Chapter 2:

No Hero: The evolution of a Navy Seal by Mark Owen

Chapter 3:

https://www.cbsnews.com/news/green-berets-the-quiet-professionals/

History Channel Vault Documentary, *History of the Green Berets*

https://sofrep.com/specialoperations/u-s-army-green-beret-special-forces-the-complete-guide/

Chapter 4:

Lone Survivor by Marcus Luttrell

https://www.navy.mil/MEDAL-OF-HONOR-RECIPIENT-MICHAEL-P-MURPHY/

https://murphsealmuseum.org/

https://www.usamm.com/blogs/news/the-navys-official-account-of-operation-red-wings

Chapter 5:

Lone Survivor by Marcus Luttrell
https://www.cmohs.org/medal/timeline
https://history.army.mil/moh/a-brief-history-of-moh.html
https://www.history.com/this-day-in-history/
medal-of-honor-created

Chapter 6:

https://navyseals.com/buds/
https://www.airforce.com/careers/in-demand-careers/
special-warfare
https://sofrep.com/specialoperations/u-s-army-green-be-
ret-special-forces-the-complete-guide/
https://www.military.com/special-operations/marine-
corps-marsoc-training.html
Navy SEALs: Buds Class 234 Documentary 2000

Chapter 7:

Sea Stories: My life in special operations by Admiral William
McRaven
https://www.fox29.com/news/i-can-hear-you-the-rest-of-
the-world-hears-you-george-w-bushs-bullhorn-speech
*Jesus Through Middle Eastern Eyes: Cultural Studies in the
Gospels* (January 22, 2008) by Kenneth Bailey

Chapter 8:

SAS Rogue Warriors, BBC Studios 2017 Matthew
Whiteman
Chapter 9:
https://pattillmanfoundation.org/
https://www.history.com/this-day-in-history/
pat-tillman-killed-by-friendly-fire-in-afghanistan

Chapter 10:

Black Hawk Down (2002 Mark Bowden, Ken Nolan, Ridley Scott)
https://www.smithsonianmag.com/history/legacy-black-hawk-down-180971000/
https://jeffstruecker.com/
www.fatherly.com
https://www.warhistoryonline.com/instant-articles/battle-of-mogadishu-heroes-gary-gordon-and-randall-shughart.html?chrome=1

Chapter 11:

https://www.psychiatry.org/patients-families/ptsd/what-is-ptsd
https://www.cdc.gov/traumaticbraininjury/index.html#:~:text=A%20traumatic%20brain%20injury%2C%20or,health%20outcomes%20after%20the%20injury.

About the Author

Drew Alan Hall is a teacher and pastor in Gadsden, Alabama. He holds a bachelor's degree from Jacksonville State University and a master's degree from Samford University. He has a passion for preaching the gospel. He loves Alabama football, Atlanta Braves baseball, and working out. He and his wife Gena have two daughters, Emory Kate and Sadie Drew.